FORGOTTEN

CHICAGO

AIRFIELDS

NICHOLAS C. SELIG

To Bob,
Happy Landings
Nick
Oct 15

Charleston London

THE
Hiſtory
PRESS

Published by The History Press
Charleston, SC 29403
www.historypress.net

First published 2014

Manufactured in the United States

ISBN 978.1.62619.554.7

Library of Congress CIP data applied for.

CONTENTS

CONTENTS

INTRODUCTION

Years from now, if some archaeological team were to begin digging through the ancient ruins of Chicago, some of the items they might discover would surely include a few of the many nuts, bolts and screws I have lost during my career as an aircraft mechanic, not to mention a number of screwdrivers, wrenches and sockets. Multiply that by the number of small airports (approximately forty-five) that once surrounded the Chicago area, and the archaeologists could find enough lost gear to fill a good-sized museum.

I'm going to make it easy for our future historians and excavators by putting as much as possible in this second volume of *Forgotten Chicago Airfields*. The sites included here exist under the suburbs of Chicago—so future archaeologists will know where to dig.

Many of these small grass-field airports date back to the post–World War I decades of the 1920s and '30s, also known as the Jazz Age. Thousands of World War I pilots couldn't shake off the thrill of flying. They became gypsy flyers, sometimes known as barnstormers, at county fairs. Some flew the airmail, which eventually evolved into an airline industry. Even the great stock market crash of 1929 only slowed but did not entirely kill the boom in aviation launched in 1927, when airmail pilot Charles Lindbergh spanned the Atlantic Ocean solo. Some barnstormers settled down and became FBOs (fixed base operators), about whom you will read later on.

In the first half of the twentieth century, aviation was an exciting and adventurous field of endeavor. Radio, movies, pulp magazines and newspaper comic strips featured the thrilling adventures of fictional characters patterned after real-life celebrities in the newspapers and newsreels of the day, such as Howard Hughes, Jimmie Doolittle, Roscoe Turner, Eddie Rickenbacker, Lindbergh and hundreds of others. Men and women from all walks of life would save nickels and dimes to afford fifteen or thirty minutes of flying time in Piper Cubs to experience the same excitement and challenge as these famous flyers. When money became tight, these small country airfields became hangouts—a home away from home, a place to trade flying tales and "hangar fly." Many lifelong friendships were established and families started here. Most would never do more than a few solo flights before settling down to jobs and families, but they would never forget that first solo flight.

Let me give you an example of how intoxicated some people are with aviation. The lowest job in the airline industry has probably always been the person who services the lavatories, dating back to the "Dizzy-Three" (Douglas DC-3) days. One particular lavatory truck driver was called "Sloppy Joe," partly because no one could pronounce his name and partly because of his ineptness at operating the pumps and hoses used to empty and refill the lavatories, resulting in many spills on the ramp as well as on himself. Joe had a rich vocabulary of swear words, which he employed whenever he had an accident. "If you hate this job so much, why don't you quit?" he was often asked. His reply: "What, an' get outta' aviation?"

So that's likely why these small FBOs struggled along for years, barely making a living, until the land was bought by a developer—but only if they owned the land and had paid the taxes. Most only leased the land and had to move on to another airport or retire. Probably the biggest boom in the business occurred with the enactment of the Civilian Pilot Training Program (CPTP) in 1939 and the GI Bill flight-training program after World War II. The CPTP helped to enable this country to build the greatest air force the world has ever seen. The postwar GI Bill was responsible for the majority of today's airline pilots after the World War II veterans approached retirement.

Included in this, as well as the previous, volume of *Forgotten Chicago Airfields* are some of our own adventures in the general aviation world as my wife, Suzette, and I have experienced them. So enjoy, and remember, if history is not recorded, it becomes a mystery. Keep 'em flyin', and happy landings!

A TALE OF TWO AIRPORTS

Or "I'll See Ya in the Funny Papers"
(a popular expression of the 1930s)

The first recorded landing of an airplane at Elmhurst Airport on Chicago's far West Side was in the spring of 1928. Mr. Sabin I. Russell had learned to fly at Langley Field, Virginia, in 1924 while with the Illinois National Guard. Lindbergh's successful solo crossing of the Atlantic in 1927 inspired him to purchase a Canadian version of the ever-popular Curtiss JN-4, which could be had for a pittance after the War to End All Wars. Russell staked it down at the northwest corner of Lake Street, Route 20 and Church Road. A Chicagoan, Dan Schroeder, had a lease on the field and erected a hangar in 1929.

The license number issued to Russell's plane, 2332, was immortalized, at least for a while, in a very popular comic strip of the day called *Harold Teen*, written and drawn by Carl Ed of the *Chicago Tribune*. Harold Teen was

Harold Teen comic strip. *Elmhurst Historical Society.*

"The gang" at Elmhurst Airport, 1930s. *Elmhurst Historical Society.*

a teenager of the Jazz Age sporting bell-bottom trousers (not seen again until the 1970s). His girlfriend was his "Sheba," and he was her "Sheik," as in the very popular silent movie starring Rudolf Valentino. So of course, Harold, being very up to date, is shown taking his "Flapper" for a jaunt in the blue, and Russell's numbers are prominent on the aerial flyer. This was the environment in which the Elmhurst Airport began. And this is how it became two airports.

Besides the funny papers, other widely read publications of the day—still around today—were *Popular Mechanics* and *Popular Science*. The advertisement sections of these magazines were chock-full of ways to get ahead in the world. One of these was the Greer School of Aviation, headed by Edwin Greer, at 2024 South Wabash in Chicago. Greer originally trained auto mechanics, but an operator at Elmhurst, Jack Rose, persuaded him to get into aviation. Greer Airways was created and established operations at Elmhurst, as well as Wilson Airport, for one season. However, Greer and Elmhurst manager Dan Schroder did not see eye to eye, so Greer negotiated for land to the west of the airport. This became Greer Airport and Greer College of Aviation. They offered flight lessons, flight services and mechanical services.

An advertisement in the Elmhurst newspapers offered complete ground course and flying lessons in new 1929 Waco and Ryan airplanes at three airports. Some people say there was a fence between the two fields, but more likely the dividing line was Church Road. By the end of the 1930s, the dual airports came to an end. The east-side airport, Elmhurst, closed, and Greer Airport became the one and only Elmhurst Airport.

There is much more to the Elmhurst story, but that's another story (or two). However, one interesting item remains. When the field closed in 1956, the Kingery Highway Route 83 was the western border. But this was not built until 1940, and until then, Salt Creek was where the field ended. With the coming of the Kingery, an engineering marvel for its day was built. This was a cloverleaf intersection at Lake Street that was probably the first such highway structure in the area, although it is commonplace now. In fact, as you cruise north on the 290 Interstate, you'll encounter a spaghetti bowl of cloverleaf as you pass over the old airport just prior to Route 83.

What would Harold Teen say? Well, he would probably be found at the Sugar Bowl Malt Shop dancing the fox-trot to a popular song of the day that went, as best as I can remember: "Everybody loves my baby, but my baby don't love nobody but me, that's plain to see. She's got a form like Venus. Honest, I ain't talkin' Greek. No one can come between us; she's my Sheba, I'm her Sheik."

Old airports and old songs. They always go together.

ARLINGTON HEIGHTS AIRPORT

In April 1942, the *Chicago Tribune* announced that the navy was considering establishment of what was to become the largest inland pilot-training base in northwestern Cook County. According to unofficial sources, the article went on to say, "enormous expansion of the Curtiss field training base at Glenview, creation of an entirely new training base on 1,100 acres near Arlington Heights, and creation of from six to eight small practice airports nearby will be administrated as one air training center." One of these small practice fields, which eventually numbered fifteen, of course became the Arlington Heights Airport. Its location was given in a postwar newspaper advertisement as "Central Road, 1 mile west of Arlington Heights Road, 3 miles west of Northwest Highway (U.S. 14), 1½ miles south of the Arlington race track, Phone: Arl. Hgts. 260." Not bad directions for those pre-GPS days.

Maurice Fishman, who became the manager of the field, was a Luscombe airplane dealer and perhaps a member of the Civil Air Patrol. A *Chicago Tribune* article and photo dated 1946 notes that the "first Civil Air Patrol plane to land at the Douglas airport [later O'Hare] was piloted by Mrs. Erlyne Conel and Miss Ruth Spietz, both Lieutenants in the CAP." Civilian airplanes belonging to CAP members were permitted to be tied down at the Douglas Airport on the air force ramp and remained there until the airlines moved from Midway in the 1960s.

Ex-GIs and civilians were encouraged to "LEARN TO FLY" in a Luscombe Silvaire for only $2,495; low-cost lessons were offered to civilians and no-cost

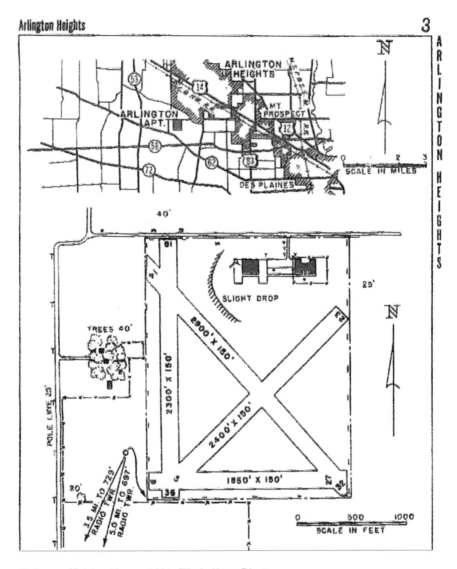

Arlington Heights Airport, 1954. *Illinois Airport Directory.*

lessons to veterans through the GI Bill. Private airplane owners were invited to rent tie-down or hangar space for nominal rates and allowed to work on their own planes. This was not always allowed at some airports. And apparently, shower and locker privileges were available in the ex-barracks. Of all the Glenview satellite fields, Arlington had the most elaborate structures. A World War II photo shows a large hangar on the east side along Central

Road with a two-story addition, including a control tower on the south side. To the east, on the other side of a parade ground, a two-story, *H*-shaped building is shown, most likely the barracks.

Unfortunately, these ideal conditions did not last very long. In fact, of the three satellite fields bred by Glenview that survived into the postwar era, Arlington Heights was the first to bite the dust. And it wasn't even suburban development that did it in; it was the U.S. Army! Here is how it happened.

Since 1947, the field had been operated by the Illinois Aircraft Services and Sales Company with Maurice Fishman as manager. When the navy declared the field surplus at the end of the war, the Village of Arlington Heights was outmaneuvered in its desire to have its own municipal airport by parties in Washington who allowed the navy to lease the property to Illinois Aircraft Services and Sales instead of to the village. What followed, according to newspaper articles of the period, was a situation in which the airport apparently generated more income for its managers by easing the postwar housing shortage than it did as an aviation service. In 1948, the ex-navy barracks became apartments for twenty-two families with rents ranging from forty to seventy-five dollars a month. One hundred acres were also set aside for a trailer camp for one hundred family trailers at eighteen dollars each. This was a time when returning veterans were trying to raise their families and simultaneously attend school on the GI Bill.

As an interesting side note, in 1929, the Curtiss Wright Corporation negotiated with the National Jockey Club to develop a flying field next to the Arlington Park Racetrack. At the time, as related in another story, the giant Curtiss group was trying to stimulate early aviation by establishing flying fields across the nation. The Arlington field failed to bear fruit, but the one at Glenview (Curtiss/Reynolds), of course, did and became the Naval Air Station a decade later, bringing about the Arlington field. Sort of a "What came first, the chicken or the egg?" kind of thing. Arlington Heights's civic leaders missed out on two chances to have an airport, it would seem.

On October 14, 1954, the *Wheeling Herald* told the world that the Arlington Heights airport was no more. It said the airport managers, Walter Rogers and Maurice Fishman, were selling their ten airplanes and other equipment and that about six hundred residents of the nearby barracks buildings and trailer park were to move by December. This came about when the federal government terminated the civilian lease in order for the Continental Air Defense Command, Anti-Aircraft Section, to build a guided missile center on the field. Eventually, about seventeen sites known as NIKE bases (for the

Greek god of victory) sprang up around the Chicago area. Five radar towers eventually appeared on the field as well. About forty-five private aircraft based at the field would have to move to other airports such as Ravenswood, Pal-Waukee, Elmhurst and Sky Harbor. In addition, the Forest View School on the field would have to close. As one might imagine, this caused hardship for the families as they tried to find new homes in such a short time, and it was hoped the deadline would be extended.

But even before this, the little community on the airfield had problems. In May 1948, an article in the *Chicago Tribune* reported that the county health department was investigating sanitary conditions at the trailer camp and apartment development on the ex-navy field. The development, the article went on to say,

> *was operated by Illinois Aircraft Services and Sales, Inc., and Louis M. Mantyband, a partner in the law firm of Jake Avery, Democratic county chairman, was the incorporating agent and director of the corporation. Health officials said that the disposal facilities were not properly maintained and of questionable size for the number of persons now using them. Mantyband and Maurice Fishman, treasurer of the firm and manager of the property, both denied this.*

Apparently, nothing came of the charges.

A small item at the bottom of the front page of the *Wheeling Herald* on October 14, 1954, noted that the route of the proposed tri-state expressway toll road had been moved farther east so it would cross the Northwest Highway between Des Plaines and Park Ridge.

I wish I could describe more happy times at Arlington, but there seems to be little recorded history of the field. However, I was fortunate to have flown with someone who was a flight instructor there before its demise. As related to me by Carl Unger, Frank Stanger flew twenty-five missions over Europe in a B-17 during World War II and then volunteered for ten more before going home. Stanger instructed in Luscombes at Arlington and then later flew Beech 18s at Chicagoland Airport for a company called Corporate Air Transport. When they moved up to turboprop Beech KingAires, the company moved to Midway. Frank was a very calm and easygoing guy, which is probably how he made it through all those missions in Europe. Nothing seemed to rattle him. For example, while flying a planeload of executives to Iowa City one day, the right engine suddenly up and quit. The early KingAires were experiencing an icing problem in the induction system, long since remedied. The boss stuck his head in the cockpit next to Frank and asked excitedly, "Where are you going to land Frank? On the highway or maybe that open field down there?" Frank calmly turned to face the boss and said, "Iowa City." (Of course.) Flying a twin-engine Beechcraft on one engine was apparently no big deal to Frank compared to flying a shot-up B-17. Frank retired at age sixty and became a dispatcher. Tragically, he was hit by a car and killed while stepping from his own car in front of his mother's house.

The Arlington Heights Historical Society provided a significant footnote of the field's history. The same barracks buildings that housed so many postwar families at one time contained almost two hundred German prisoners of war starting in May 1944. The society's "Chronicle of a Prairie Town" stated that these POWs were members of Rommel's Afrika Corps, mostly seventeen to twenty years old. They were housed in Building H, a two-story barracks enclosed with barbed wire, with a soccer field adjacent. A guard detail of thirty-seven solders was assigned to the compound. Transported to Glenview, they performed heavy labor, grounds maintenance and also engine maintenance at a pay rate of $21.80 a month in coupons good at the prison post exchange.

Another newspaper article dated 1951 shows that Maurice Fishman was active in more aviation activities than just the Arlington Heights Airport. Chicago Public Works commissioner Hewitt recommended the concession for servicing aircraft at Chicago's lakefront airport, Meigs Field, be awarded to Fishman, of 7657 Sheridan Road, the high bidder.

Probably the last airplane to depart Arlington Heights airfield was an Army De Haviland Beaver L-20 in the 1970s. A fellow flight instructor and friend of mine at Aviation Training Enterprises at Midway Airport, Vince Palermo, ferried the Liaison plane late in the afternoon to Naper Aero Estates. Palermo, an army reservist, lived nearby and delivered it to its final destination the next day. Knowing I had been an L-20 crew chief years ago, Vince invited me to ride along, which I enjoyed very much. When the army presence ended, the airfield became a golf course with plans for a park, picnic and hiking area.

The field served the country well by training hundreds of navy pilots and later many civilian pilots. Its missiles helped keep us safe from the threat of Soviet bombers. Across Central Road now is a senior retirement residence. Kind of completes the picture, doesn't it?

ASSUME

This story takes place when airplanes sat with their tails on the ground and their noses pointing up at the sky. The participants might have been flying Cubs, Aeroncas or Taylorcrafts, maybe even some military BTs for all one knows. The incident described might have occurred more than once throughout the history of aviation, and it might occur again someday. As Fats Waller said, "One never knows, do one?"

A student pilot was droning along one fine day on his (or maybe her) first solo cross-country flight. As sometimes happened to motors in olden days (and sometimes nowadays, too), the droning suddenly ceased. Our pilot had been properly trained for just such an experience. A suitable field was picked and a safe landing made. Fortunately, this was when open farmland was plentiful and creeping suburbia had not yet begun creeping.

The student walked to a nearby farmhouse and asked to use the telephone. It hung on the wall and had a hand crank on the side. The flight school and chief instructor was contacted and advised of the location of the stricken machine.

In due time, another airplane of a similar type arrived from the school and circled the farm field. The situation was studied, and a question arose in the mind of the rescue pilot. The field in which the student's plane sat appeared rather small and was surrounded by fences on all sides. The rescue pilot, a rather junior instructor, after circling several times, decided that if a student could land safely in such a small field, so could he. The seeds of disaster had been sown.

Willie Howell's first Cub, 1938. *Tinley Park Historical Society.*

The first approach ended in a go-around. The second one, in spite of much forward slipping and fishtailing, was no better. In a do-or-die attempt, the third try was made hanging on the prop on the verge of a stall behind the power curve, with the tail wheel clipping a fence rail. On the ground but rushing at the opposite fence, the only alternative was a brake-stomping ground loop. The ship spun around just short of the fence, but centrifugal force dropped the outside wing onto the ground, ripping the wing tip fabric and tip bow.

The excited and exasperated instructor stomped over to the student and inquired, "How the blazes [or words to that effect] were you able to land in this field?"

And the student replied, "Oh, I didn't land in this field, Sir. I landed over there in the big field and bounced over the fence into this field."

Hence the title of this little tale: when you assume, you make an ass out of u and me! (Personally, I don't use that word; I'd rather arrive at a conclusion. But that's another story.)

Of such trials are some pilots made or broken. They say you can always tell a new flight instructor—but not much!

AURORA AIRWAYS AIRPORT

I'm sure many pioneering airman, mechanics and what have you once occupied this airfield, but with one or two exceptions, the most memorable recent character was a seagull.

For a short time during the 1930s, the airport was managed by John Livingston, a well-known air-racing pilot of the era. Richard Bach, one of the outstanding aviation authors of the 1970s, wrote a book about a seagull that strived for perfection in the art of flying. He named the seagull Jonathan Livingston Seagull. The book became a bestseller, and Bach went on to write many more thought-provoking flying stories.

Aurora Airways was located on the west side of the Fox River along Illinois Route 31 and just south of Exposition Park. This amusement park was founded in 1922 and was actually larger than and almost as well known as Riverview Park in Chicago. Some sources say the airfield was built to accommodate the park. The track was later known as Aurora Downs.

Opened in 1927, the field became a commercial operation in 1928 under Midwest Airways Corporation of Monmouth, Illinois, and John Livingston became director. Later in the 1940s, when Livingston was operating the school in Waterloo, Iowa, the future author Bach was a young fence hanger and airport "gofer" watching the airplanes come and go.

Between 1928 and 1933, Livingston was one of the most consistent winners in the air-racing circuit, winning $60,000 (quite a haul in Depression-era dollars) and many trophies. Starting as an auto and motorcycle mechanic, he became an aviation mechanic and soon advanced

Aurora Airways Airport, the new I-88 toll road and the Aurora Downs Racetrack, 1961. *George Miner.*

to the cockpit as a pilot when he soloed in 1920. Although starting as a mechanic with Midwest Airways Corporation, which had operations in all three cities, within five years he had become general manager. This was the era of the "Pylon Polishers" type of racing, as compared to long-distance racing. In spite of his lack of a college degree, Livingston achieved greater speed with his aircraft with many small modifications rather than an increase in horsepower.

So now we come to one of the "exceptions" with which I started this story: Robert F. Luman. I met Mr. Luman back in the 1970s when I was a flight instructor and maintenance manager for Monty Montgomery's Aviation Training Enterprises, Inc., operating out of Midway Airport (known now as American Flyers). He was a very soft-spoken and easygoing guy and ran a clean and efficient shop. This was at the present Aurora Airport at Sugar Grove. How Mr. Luman and his family bridged the ten miles from Aurora to Sugar Grove is an interesting story.

Luman began his aviation career in the late 1930s at the Joliet Airport, where he also met his future wife. He was a good mechanic and could fix anything. During World War II, he worked for two years at the Joliet Arsenal. (Today, this area is the location of the Lincoln Veterans Cemetery, a very large transportation center and the Joliet Auto Racetrack. However, the railroad tracks connecting the underground ammunition bunkers and some buildings are still visible.) Luman then worked at the Lewis School of Aeronautics at Lockport (now Lewis University) and probably obtained his

Aurora Industrial Airpark, 1960s. *Aurora Historical Society.*

Airplane & Engine Certificate there. Sometime in the late 1940s or early 1950s, he moved to the original Aurora Airport, which went by several name changes and configurations, according to the *Illinois Airport Directories*. A 1946 survey made by a commission researching sites for a replacement for Midway Airport described the Aurora Airport on Illinois Route 31 as an all-turf field, 2,350 by 1,242 feet, with adequate drainage and room for expansion to the south and west. Twenty-one airplanes were based there, and transportation was provided by two railroads and a bus line.

The 1954 airport directory, which was hand drawn, shows a unique runway layout for the day and age. There were two sets of parallel runways, still turf, running north–south and east–west with cultivated areas in between. A large hanger was in the northwest corner with a smaller T-type hangar to the east of it. The Chicago, Burlington and Quincy (CB&Q) Railroad ran down the east side of the field next to Route 31, and trees, a road and phone lines, together with a 150-foot-high tank, bordered the north edge. The operator and manager was Peter L. Julius.

Later directories contained actual aerial photographs with the racetrack to the north and listed Pete Julius still in charge. However, the 1958 photo shows the excavations taking place between the airport and the racetrack for the coming east–west toll road, I-88.

So you would imagine that the coming of the toll road would spell the end of the airport, right? Well, yes and no. Through some clever and convoluted manipulations by the parties involved, in 1954, airport operator Peter Julius, the original owner of the ninety-acre airfield, persuaded a group of local industrialists to buy the thirty-three acres containing the sod landing strips and hangars. They then turned the land over to the city free of charge, which made the airport a municipal facility and eligible for state aid in paving the main east–west runway. Julius continued to operate the airport while holding title to the remaining fifty-seven acres surrounding it.

In 1957, the Illinois Toll Highway Commission agreed to buy the thirty-three acres owned by Aurora and pay damages for loss of the airport. It also agreed to buy fourteen acres of the land owned by Julius, who was paid damages for the loss of the airport business. Julius took part of the settlement in cash and twenty-seven acres of the Aurora Airport property, including the landing strip. He also bought back the hangar and administration building for 10 percent of their value, the usual price asked for buildings the purchaser would have to tear down. So Julius was paid for a business he never really lost, which he turned into an Industrial Air Park. Aurora received sufficient compensation from the toll road and matching funds from the government so it could build a new airport near Sugar Grove in 1960.

By 1964, Bob Luman was listed as operator and manager of the old Aurora Airport; he moved to the Sugar Grove Airport in 1966 and passed on in the mid-1990s. At the present time, the third generation of the Luman family are among the leading and oldest operators at the present Aurora Airport. At the entrance to the air facilities, in front of the number one parking space, is a sign that reads: "Reserved for Ma Luman." However, reserved she is not; she is a very outgoing, spry and enjoyably talkative lady of ninety-five with a remarkable memory. Sons Bob Jr. and Mike run a much bigger operation than the one I first saw in the 1970s. A third son, George, died during an air show in 1975. Much more could be written about this family, but that's another story

Keep 'em flyin', Lumans!

DE KALB AIRPORT

Although many, if not most, of the lost airports of the Chicago area played some small part in the winning of World War II, the De Kalb Airport, which still exists today but in a greatly altered form, started in a most mysterious way. The work performed there was classified top secret, and the people employed were sworn to secrecy for more than twenty years after the end of the war.

Prior to World War II, a local man, Pete Taylor, established a flying service on the outskirts of De Kalb, at one time along Kenslinger Road and at another time on Crego Road. With only a small wooden building and a Piper J-3 Cub, he provided tie-down spaces along the sod runway and gave rides and instruction. Later came charter flights, aircraft parts sales and crop dusting.

On September 26, 1942, the *De Kalb Daily Chronicle* announced several important news items to the citizens of the mostly farming area fifty miles west of Chicago. The German drive on Stalingrad was slowing. A grainy black-and-white photograph on the front page showed a U.S. Flying Fortress bomber attacking Japanese ships in the Solomon Islands. Also, the new aircraft carrier *Lexington*, named in honor of the ship sunk in the Battle of the Coral Sea, was launched more than a year ahead of schedule. And a program of gas rationing was announced for the nation's twenty-seven million civilian motorists, along with a thirty-five-mile-per-hour speed limit. But the banner headline of the newspaper shouted, "NAVY PLANES TO BE BUILT IN DE KALB."

Navy hangar, De Kalb Airport, 1950s. *Tom Cleveland.*

Navy hangar, De Kalb Airport, 1960s. *Tim Coltrin.*

The article went on to say that major shares of the city's manufacturing resources were to be used to produce a new airplane for the U.S. Navy. The Rudolph Wurlitzer Company had been determined to be the leader in the country in the handling of wood and manufacturing of wood products and therefore was the reason for the navy's decision to make De Kalb the center of a tremendous production plan. The Wurlitzer Company was to be the major subcontractor for the Interstate Aircraft and Engineering Corporation of El Segundo, California, which designed the plane. The government had purchased the Arlington Furniture Company to be leased to the Interstate Aircraft

Navy TDR-3 drone, 1944. Air Trails *magazine.*

Corporation. This huge factory, which had the longest furniture assembly line in the country, was to be used to assemble the type of aircraft to be built there.

It was also announced that the navy would soon secure land near the factory for an airfield and large hangar that would be entirely fenced and guarded around the clock. In the meantime, De Kalb would be expected to develop the necessary housing, recreation and transportation for the large workforce that soon would be needed, 50 percent of whom were expected to be female.

Five hundred aircraft were contracted to be built, and almost two hundred were utilized by the navy in the Pacific campaign against the Japanese on the island of Rabaul. What was so unique, and therefore so secretive, about these aircraft was the fact that they were radio-controlled, pilotless drones capable of carrying two-thousand-pound bombs. A radio and television camera was mounted in the nose and directed by another plane to the target. About fifty drone missions were launched in September 1944. Television had been introduced to the public at the 1939 World's Fair, but civilian use was put off until after the war.

The TDR-1s, as they were designated, were twin-engine, low-wing monoplanes, thirty-six feet long with fifty-foot wingspans and spindly fixed landing gear. Small cockpits were provided for test flights but of course were empty on their final missions. There was no intention of imitating the Japanese suicide missions. The electronics of the day were in the early stages of development, and the missions were not always successful. A similar mission was used in the European theater of operations, utilizing four-engine bombers packed with explosives. As they were not equipped for remote-control takeoff as were the TDR-1s, the flight crews were to get the bombers airborne and then parachute to safety while directing bombers controlled the now drone aircraft to the target. Tragically, on one mission, the bomber exploded before the pilots could bail out. One of the pilots was Joseph P. Kennedy, brother of President John F. Kennedy.

These early experiments with electronic guidance and control by television finally came to fruition with the guided missiles of the 1990s in the Gulf War.

After the war ended, the airport, which was called "Interstate," was purchased by the City of De Kalb, and Pete Taylor became part of the operation. With his leadership, the airport became a center of freight, charter and executive flight operations. He welcomed the Boy Scouts and Girl Scouts to the field for free rides and belonged to the Illinois Flying Farmers, the Aircraft Owners and Pilots Association and the Experimental Aircraft Association and supported the 99s, the Women's Flying Organization. He became a De Kalb alderman and served on many city committees. He was also a Piper aircraft dealer and, after retirement, developed a widely known aircraft parts business.

The first time I met Pete Taylor was during the first rebuilding of our family's Stinson Flying Station Wagon. The original Bendix wheel brake assemblies were inadequate when the plane was new and were now in need of updated units. Pete took me to a large barn somewhere near the airport that was jam-packed with airplane parts. Up in a loft, he showed me the wheel and brake assembles from a Piper Tri-Pacer, including tires and tubes. They were hydraulically operated shoe and drum brakes and fit perfectly on the Stinson. They worked quite well for many years until we updated again with Cleveland brakes. During that same decade of the 1970s, I had several occasions to rent a flatbed trailer from Pete. I was, at that time, the maintenance manager for a nationwide flight school, and it was occasionally necessary to recover aircraft that were damaged in windstorms and a few emergency landings. (And that's another interesting story.)

Suzette and I enjoyed many fly-in breakfasts at De Kalb in the large wooden hangar built by the navy in 1942. The breakfasts were usually held by the local—and one of the oldest—EAA chapter in the area and still are to this day. The hangar always housed many interesting kinds of aircraft. The stairs leading up to the small control tower were blocked off, as they were quite old and unsafe by that time. On each side of the hangar was a brick office, and in one of them was a C-3 Link trainer, again of World War II vintage. If I remember correctly, it was owned by the State of Illinois Department of Aeronautics but operated by Civil Air Patrol volunteers and was available free of charge to pilots to maintain proficiency in instrument flying. The 3,800- by 50-foot east–west runway was connected to the hangar and ramp area on the west side by a 750- by 50-foot taxiway. The runway and taxiway appeared to be the same, only the runway had gravel lining both sides. There always seemed to be either a north or south wind blowing whenever the fly-ins were held, and some of the arrivals provided great entertainment along with the pancakes and sausages. Quite often, a crop-duster plane could be seen arriving or departing on the taxiway regardless of the wind direction. Time was money in that business.

Until recently, there had been a non-directional low-frequency beacon (209 on the dial, Dah Dit Dit—Dah Dit Dah—Dah Dit Dit Dit, DKB) on the field, one of the few in the area. By the late 1980s, the navy hangar had been torn down, and a ramp was built on the east side of the field where the fly-ins are held now. A new east–west runway with a parallel taxiway and a northeast-southwest runway make the field visible from miles away now. De Kalb has now entered the corporate jet age, and the field has been named in Pete Taylor's honor. But it all came into being during a time of great need by our nation. Thankfully, it did not become one of the Chicago area's many lost airports.

For more information on radio-controlled aircraft in World War II, see *Shoot Only at the Red Aircraft*, by Bill Coons, published in 2007.

CLOW INTERNATIONAL AIRPORT

At one time, when the area was all cornfields, there were two RLA's (Restricted Landing Areas) south of Clow International Airport in what is now Bolingbrook, Illinois. Clow itself was also only a grass-strip RLA until it went commercial in 1973. Then the east–west grass runway became a taxiway, and the north–south strip was paved. Prior to that, however, the Chicago Glider Club operated off the east–west strip. The first RLA south belonged to Richard and Mary Alice Lambert on a gravel road off Washington Street (now Weber Road) at what is now 115th Street. They were members of the Flying Farmers Association, as were many of the local farmers, and participated in the yearly Wheatland Plowing Match along Route 59 north of Plainfield. The field had two wooden hangars (which still stand), containing a half dozen planes and a 2,265-foot grass north–south runway. About a half mile south of Lambert and in almost a direct line was Ronald W. George's (Mary Alice's brother) RLA. Also grass and aligned north–south at 2,300 feet, it had one large wooden hangar. Two of the planes based there were unique. One was a red open-cockpit biplane, maybe a Waco, that belonged to Marcellus Foose. He was the "F" in B&F Aircraft Supply on 95th Street in Oak Lawn, which started at Harlem Airport in 1937. The other plane was a home-built scale replica of a World War I SE-5 fighter. It was built by American Airlines flight engineer Bob Zilinsky and is still flying in the twenty-first century.

Going back to Lambert, the only two planes I was acquainted with were a Stinson (of course) and a B-25 Mitchell bomber (believe it or not!). The

Glider Club at Clow International Airport, 1960s. *Mel Finzer.*

Boyd Clow's Navion and John Daly's Eagle in front of the old restaurant, Clow International Airport, 1995. *Author's collection.*

bomber was flown in about 1970 and sat in the weeds until about 1981. After some restoration, it was flown out but suffered engine failure and had to return. It eventually made it to Rockford, Illinois, where it was fully restored, and is now flying the air show circuit.

What I remember most about these three fields was a little excursion one day when my good buddy Mel Finzer and I were out airport hopping in

Mel Finzer, Boyd Clow and Pal, 2005. *Mel Finzer.*

his J-3 Cub. We took off from Clow to the south, cut the power and glided down to a landing at Lambert. We made a touch-and-go and did the same thing at George, another touch-and-go. The wind was calm, so we made a "crop dusters" turn (a 90-degree left and a 270-degree right) and did the same thing going north. After a touch-and-go at each, it was back to Clow. We probably stopped for a hot dog at Lou's hot dog stand, run by Lou and Elmer Hess and located in a corner of one of the hangars. This was before the first restaurant was built along Washington Street, which is now Webber Road. We celebrated five takeoffs and landings at three different airports in ten or fifteen minutes. Try that nowadays!

The two airports south of Clow and another grass field called Plainfield, farther west next to the I-55 toll road (old Route 66), were all in the same family, more or less. Mary Alice Lambert, who runs a nice little gift shop in Plainfield, told me Plainfield was owned by her cousin, Forest George.

The 1958 *Illinois Airport Directory* lists an RLA two miles east of Plainfield under the name of Forest George. In 1962, the Plainfield-George Field was managed by Carl Taylor and operated by Norm Wolf and Nick Kucki. (These three fellows were the basis of many local tales.) Nick Kucki later moved to Clow but ended up at Lake Village in Indiana. I'm not sure if the

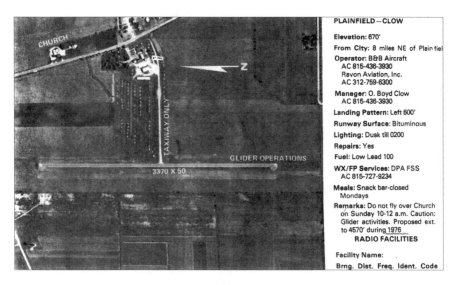

Clow International Airport, 1962. *Illinois Airport Directory.*

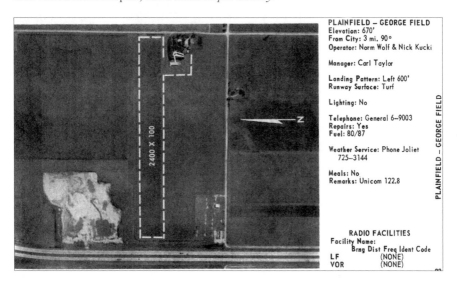

Plainfield, George RLA, 1962. *Illinois Airport Directory.*

Carl Taylor mentioned above was the same fellow who later operated at Midway Airport in the 1970s, but if so, he was also quite a character.

Dick Hill, in his book *The Bird Aircraft History*, published in 2004, describes the airport along I-55 in some detail. Wolf and Kucki, Hill notes, originally worked at the Ford plant on south Cicero Avenue in Chicago (also the home of the Tucker automobile and later a shopping mall), building P&W R-4360 engines for B-36 bombers. They formed a partnership and rented a stall at Forrest George's airstrip at Plainfield, relicensing and repairing planes.

Clow International (so named because of all the different ethnic backgrounds of the pilots who were based there) fortunately has not become a lost airport, at least not entirely. Only half the original airport exists today, so you might say it's only half lost. The eastern half along Webber Road was developed in the late 1990s into a large food store, a home improvement store, various restaurants and shops and even a movie theater—all within walking distance, although an airport car is available. This all came about at the same time a large city to the east was destroying its beautiful lakefront airport in the middle of the night. Joe De Paulo, a Naperville builder, purchased the airport from Oliver Boyd Clow in 1999. He so enjoyed it that he learned to fly and decided to keep the west half of the field with the runway as an amenity for the community. He later sold the airport to another forward-thinking man, the mayor of Bolingbrook, Roger Claar. Together they developed the Illinois Aviation Museum on the field and a very popular restaurant facing the runway. And all this started when a farmer, Boyd Clow, traded a tractor for an airplane back in the 1950s, learned to fly and started allowing a few friends to tie down their airplanes there.

Many more stories could be told by the many characters hanging out at the new restaurant who used to gather at a run-down trailer, the former Glider Club office. But that's another story.

You can catch a glimpse of the old Clow International Airport and Boyd himself in a hilarious flying sequence from a 1980 movie with Tom Selleck and Don Ameche called *Folks!*. You can learn a lot watching old movies.

ELMHURST GOES DOWN IN FLAMES

I don't want to set the world on fire; I just want to start a flame in your heart.
—*The Ink Spots,* Your Hit Parade, *1940*

In the fall of 1956, the U.S. Army and I parted company. As related elsewhere, I had been trained as an aircraft mechanic and served as a crew chief on several liaison-type aircraft for most of my three-year enlistment. Armed with a glowing letter of recommendation from my former first sergeant, I obtained a job at Elmhurst Airport on Lake Street, Route 20 and Highway 83. The manager of the field was Art Fisher, the main operator was Tufts-Edgecombe and others leasing space were Lloyd Flying Service, George Priester and the Moody Bible Institute. At least fifty airplanes were based on the grass field with four turf runways. A right-hand traffic pattern was advised for the south and southwest runways due to a five-hundred-foot-high radio tower a half mile east of the field.

But I was unaware of all of this when I answered the advertisement in the *Chicago Tribune* placed by another operator on the field, B&M Aircraft. Brunke and McGee ran a maintenance and repair service in two wooden hangars on Lake Street. I had been working there for about six weeks when, one cold December morning, I was assigned to the dope and fabric shop in the most westerly of the two hangars. As I stepped into the dim hangar from the bright outdoors, I saw a brand-new Piper Tri-Pacer. When my eyes adjusted to the light, a small puddle of gasoline was discernible beneath the plane. Then I heard the clatter of an extension lamp falling to the floor and the *pop!* of the light bulb. Instantly, the puddle was aflame. I ran to the adjacent hangar for a fire extinguisher and back again. In that short time, the entire interior of the hangar had caught fire, including the walls, the ceiling and the Tri-Pacer, which was now just a tubular skeleton.

I ran outside again and started helping to push aircraft away from the inferno. An ex-military Fairchild PT-19 was stuck and wouldn't move. Thinking the parking brake was set, someone jumped aboard and pulled a likely looking *T* handle. A cloud of white steam hissed out from under the engine compartment. Someone shouted, "The heat is getting to the gas tanks! She's going to blow up!" Everyone ran like the dickens until the guy in the cockpit yelled, "It's only the CO2 fire extinguisher! I pulled it by mistake!"

Meanwhile, fifty-five-gallon drums of paint and solvents stored outside along the hangar wall started erupting, the tops blowing off like Roman candles. A red-cabin Waco biplane sat next to the hangar sans wings. They were in the hangar, having just been repaired and re-covered with new fabric. The fuselage and tail feathers were saved, but the wings were gone, along with everything else in the hangar.

Again, I was not aware of it, but a high-tension power line was scheduled to be erected across the airport the next summer, and all planes were to be off the field by the end of the year. B&M had plans to move to Elgin and asked me to do likewise. It was only another fifteen miles down the road on Lake Street. And I did move for a while, but that's another story.

By the way, that Tri-Pacer was covered with a new product called "Butyrate," which was supposed to be less inclined to burn.

About thirty years later, I was asked to speak at one of the monthly meetings of the Suburban Aviation Club. This club had originated in the area of the Hinsdale Airport, and Suzette and I had recently become members. After I finished my story of the closing of Elmhurst, a fellow in the audience asked if I remembered him. I said, "No, I'm afraid not." He announced that he was the fellow we had left in the cockpit of the Fairchild, which we had abandoned so hastily when we thought it was about to blow up in our faces. Before I could get his name, someone interrupted, and when I later tried to find him, he had disappeared. I hope I don't have to wait another thirty years to meet him again.

FIELD OF FIFTEEN

The Satellite Airfields of Glenview NAS

Although it was common practice to situate practice airfields around large military air bases throughout the country during World War II, the airfields surrounding the Glenview Naval Air Station (NAS) are the basis of this story for many reasons. They certainly fit under the title of forgotten airfields, and most of them were unique, if only in name.

Arlington Heights, Wood Dale and Chicagoland at Half Day became commercial fields after the war, but Schumburg did not begin operations until the 1970s and originally was called Roselle. Indeed, the present Schumburg Airport and the location of the "Schaunberg" satellite field depicted on the 1945 area map provided by Dick Ferron appear to be two different sites. Two different road intersections are given for Schumburg. One is at Irving and Rodenberg Roads and the other at Barrington Road between Irving and Golf Roads. With the advent of the Elgin-O'Hare Expressway (which doesn't go to either Elgin or O'Hare yet), the topography has been altered quite a bit.

A fourth field at Libertyville is perhaps the oddball of the bunch. It was the only field with concrete runways. The 1954 *Illinois Airport Directory* depicts it with three runways in a triangular pattern, each about 2,300 feet by 150 feet, four miles south of Libertyville and west of Deerfield, in the apex of Highways 45 and 21. It was marked as "CLOSED, DO NOT LAND," and the operator was the Air Defense Command. It was possibly a NIKE site and, when later abandoned, became an unofficial drag-racing site until steel cables were strung across the runways. About 1973, the Northbrook

Dick Lloyd's Cherokee in front of the old restaurant, Roselle Airport. *Bill Lloyd.*

Air racer Florence Klingensmith, Curtiss/Reynolds Airport, 1930. *Rudy Profant collection.*

Omni Directional Range Station was moved from Chicagoland Airport to the Libertyville site.

So that leaves eleven satellite fields situated in a fifteen-mile arc around the NAS from the southwest to the north-northwest. Some were named for the nearby town or village. Others were so far out in the boondocks that they acquired very peculiar names, such as Murphy's Circus near Routes 59 and 72, Prall's Pit near Central Road and Barrington Road and Sporlin along Route 83, south of Route 22 and north of Dundee Road.

Dennis O'Brien was a primary flight instructor at Glenview NAS in 1944. At the age of ninety and still living in Chicago's West Side suburbs, he was able to relate some little-known details of primary flight instruction at Glenview during the war. A student at DePaul University before the war, O'Brien

Modern airports. *Curtiss/Wright publication* Trade Winds, *1930.*

learned to fly at Lewis Holy Name School of Aeronautics at Lockport, Illinois. Entering the WTS (War Training Service), the wartime extension of the CPTP (Civilian Pilot Training Program), he took ground school at Loyola and rode a station wagon to Lewis daily to fly. After completing the advanced course in aerobatics in a Waco UPF-7, he was qualified to instruct at Glenview.

As many as thirty or forty training flights would leave Glenview every morning and return at noon to repeat the same routine in the afternoon. The Stearman training planes had no radios, so landings and takeoffs were made in parallel on the big field into whatever direction the wind blew. O'Brien always tried to take his students to the closest field, usually Arlington Heights. There was a standard approach funnel leaving and returning to the field. This was along the east–west road between St. Mary's School and the CCC (Civilian Conservation Corp) camp along the Des Plaines River at eight hundred feet altitude. The outlying fields were fenced off to keep livestock and people safe from the aircraft practicing takeoffs and landings. In addition, every day a truck was sent to each field with a mechanic and his toolbox, along with a fire extinguisher and, most important, a box lunch. O'Brien had only one mishap when his student stood his plane on its nose and bent the prop.

Air race poster, Curtiss/Reynolds field, 1930.

Army contract school Stearman trainer, Curtiss/Reynolds field, 1939. *Stan Tonkin.*

Robert Taylor was one of the many Hollywood film stars who joined the services when the war began and was also an instructor at Glenview. He and O'Brien were roommates for a while. Taylor's wife, Barbara Stanwick, also a Hollywood star, was staying at the Edgewater Beach Hotel on Chicago's north shore, so O'Brien didn't see much of Taylor most evenings. However, a training film was produced in a studio in uptown Chicago, starring, of course, Robert Taylor. Although he never got any film credit, O'Brien's hands and feet were seen showing the correct placement of the airplane controls, while Taylor's head and shoulders appeared in the Stearman's cockpit. Another star in the film was Alfalfa from the *Our Gang* comedy series of the 1930s. His character was the Dilbert who showed the wrong way to do everything.

The sailors who manned the outlying flying fields had lonely jobs at times. They had to be there in good weather and bad. Some caught up on their sleep; others played solitaire (with real playing cards, no computers yet), while budding writers composed stories and poems. The base newspaper contained a line from the Schumburg site that commented: "The wind sure does howl and blow out this way and loneliness sometimes gets you, but we overcome this by holding discussions on current events…with the field mice."

Although many more stories are now gone with the people who could have related them, one particular mystery has remained unsolved throughout my research. On the 1945 area map depicting the fifteen satellite airfields, there are nine circles with three red triangles inside them. Not one of the many people I've talked to knows what these are supposed to represent. But then, all good ghost stories are supposed to end that way, right?

HAEDTLER FIELD

The Other Airport with Three Names

This little grass field was once along Governors Highway near Richton Park and Park Forest, about thirty miles south of the Chicago Loop. Although I had flown over the field a few times, the only time I ever landed there was during a Civil Air Patrol Search and Rescue mission in early October 1976. About twelve private airplanes and pilots answered the call for volunteers, including four from our residential airstrip near Naperville. Along with our 1948 Stinson Flying Station Wagon were a 1940 Cessna Airmaster, a 1960 Cessna 172 and a Piper Comanche. A Cessna Cardinal, based at the Frankfort Airport, had been reported missing that Monday morning when the pilot failed to report for work. After assembling at the field, we were paired up with observers, and we headed out to our assigned search areas.

It was a warm, sunny Monday afternoon, and my observer and I agreed to look carefully at each cornfield we flew over en route to our assigned grid. The corn was about eight feet tall that fall, and we felt sure any downed airplane could be seen only from directly above. This was exactly what turned out to be the case. Before we were halfway to our assigned grid, we spotted the Cardinal upside down in a cornfield near Peotone, Illinois, about five hundred feet from Interstate 57 and an equal distance from a farmhouse in the other direction. We reported the location to base by radio (a Narco Omnigator with four crystals) as we circled. We learned that was not a good idea. Almost immediately, we were almost run over by two other aircraft anxious to get a gander at the wreck. It was necessary to guide the state

Above: Marty Haedtler, Guadalcanal, 1942. Tribune *photo*.

Left: Marty and Ruth Haedtler, 1960s. *Ted Koston*.

police into the proper cornfield because they couldn't see the plane from the Interstate. We discovered later that the nearby farmer had heard a loud noise on the night of the crash, Saturday, but could not see anything because of the tall corn and the fog, which was probably the cause of the accident.

The pilot had been thrown from the wreckage and was dead. The passenger, a young lady, was injured and had hung by her seatbelt upside down for thirty-three hours before rescue workers reached her. A cold front passed through the area that night. I'm sure the girl would not have survived much longer.

The antenna for the ELT (emergency location transmitter) was mounted on top of the Cardinal, of course, and was jammed into the dirt beneath the plane, smothering its transmission. The ELTs are battery operated and activated by a *G* switch when an aircraft comes to a sudden stop—sometimes even during a hard landing. They were mandated into law by Congress, not the FAA, when a congressman was lost in the western mountains.

So that was my bittersweet introduction to Haetdler Field, previously known as Wings Field and originally as Governor's Air Park. The *Illinois Airport Directories* for the years the field was in operation show several operators and managers after Walt Thielman and his Midwest Aircraft Sales Company left Chicago Heights for Governors. Freeman's "Abandoned and Little Known Airfields" website covers some details of the field. He reports that the ashes of a CAP pilot, Jim Davis, were scattered by his daughter and son on the cornfield where the runways once were.

Suzette and I first met Martin C. Haedtler, "Marty," and his wife, Ruth, at their house in Oak Lawn in 1965. We had just joined Chapter 15 of the Experimental Aircraft Association (EAA), and meetings were held at their house. We learned later that it was Marty's neighbor Glenn Courtwright, across the street, who first introduced him to the EAA. (Courtwright and partner Marcellus Foose had an aircraft supply store on Ninety-fifth Street, B&F Aircraft, after their original shop at the Harlem Airport closed due to urban sprawl in the 1950s.) Sadly, the last time we saw Marty was at the first Oshkosh Fly-In in 1970. When he died in March 1971, we learned it was from wounds sustained in the crash of a Bell P-39 on the island of Guadalcanal in the early days of World War II. He was never able to pass an airman's medical exam after that, but he became an early EAA director, co-founder of the Midwest Regional Air Show involving four Chicago-area EAA chapters and built two airplanes. During the EAA Fly-Ins held in the 1960s at Rockford, Illinois, Marty was the master of ceremonies of the Evening Programs, conducted the Interview Circle and was aircraft parking chairman several times. Ruth Haetdler was registration chairman for several years.

EAA Chapter 15, now meeting at Lewis Airport in Romeoville, began awarding the Marty Haedtler Memorial Award to a member each year for outstanding performance in recognition of Marty's inspiration and teamwork. I am very proud to have known Marty and to have once flown from the small grass field that was named after him, at least for a short while. I'm sure Marty would have been proud of the accomplishments of the Civil Air Patrol there.

HARLEM AIRPORT

The Charge of the Light Brigade

In the late summer of 1938, a group of pilots in the Chicago area decided to put on an air show. They all agreed that it was nice to see the National Air Races at Cleveland and Curtiss-Reynolds up on the North Side, but there was little chance to compete with the likes of Roscoe Turner, Art Chester and Steve Wittman. It was true that the previous year's Thompson race had been won by a novice auto mechanic, Rudy Kling from nearby Lemont, but that still was not very satisfying. They wanted a show that the amateur little guy could participate in. This meant the Cubs, Aeroncas and Taylorcrafts.

These were called "light planes." Until the mid-1930s, most civilian aircraft were still large two- or three-place open-cockpit biplanes leftover from the Great War. Even the newer designs were mostly powered by Curtiss OX-5 engines of ninety horsepower that could be bought for fifty dollars still in their army crates. The radial engines, such as those that powered Lindbergh's "Spirit of St. Louis," were gradually replacing the OX-5s but were very expensive. A young German immigrant research assistant named Langewiesche paid twenty-five cents a minute for dual instruction at Chicago Municipal Airport when he could afford a half hour's time. (He became a production test pilot during the next "Great War" and wrote the greatest aviation book ever, called *Stick and Rudder*.)

So by the middle of the Great Depression, most people who could still afford to fly were raised on these "puddle jumpers" of fifty or less horsepower that rented for half the price of a big ship, usually six to eight dollars an hour. They were mostly powered by four-cylinder opposed engines made by

Bohl and Schumaker Cubs at Harlem Airport, 1950s. *Craig Mantegna.*

Continental, Lycoming or Franklin of forty- or fifty-horsepower (sixty-five-horsepower was yet to come) "flat fours," as compared to "round" engines. By limiting the show to fifty horsepower or less, everyone would have a chance to show his or her stuff. This was not to be a death-defying racing show around pylons like the big boys (and girls). It was to be a safe and sane show for fun, organized and run by the private plane owners and sportsman pilots of the Chicago area to sell aviation, and especially light plane aviation, to the public.

But where? This is where Harlem Airport comes in. At that time (1938), Harlem was way out in the wide-open spaces. Harlem Avenue was (and still is) 7200 West by Chicago's street-numbering system, nine miles west of State Street ("That Great Street") at Eighty-seventh Street and about ten miles south of Madison Street. (Eight blocks to a mile, as I was taught.) As you drive north on the Tri-State Tollway, I-294, it would have been at your three o'clock just before you cross the Sanitary Canal. The airport was managed by Fred "Shoes" Schumacher and his wife, Eleanor. They had a fleet of Cubs for rental and instruction and volunteered the field for the day. (These two and a partner named Wilbur Buhl are good for a couple more stories.)

This page: Harlem Airport aerials, 1950s. *Craig Mantegna.*

Harlem Airport, 1937. *B&F Aircraft.*

The next job was to round up some sponsors and donations for prizes. Air Associates, a nationwide warehouse of aircraft parts and accessories, donated a steerable tail wheel (tail skids were the norm), a set of navigation lights (battery operated) and a $27 Aeromarine magnetic compass. A well-known steak house and Prohibition watering hole called The Barn, run by Andrew Kluck, donated $50 dollars in prize money (this cocktail lounge and banquet room was still around in the 1990s). The Borden Milk Company (then known as the Borden-Wieland Milk Company) kicked in another $50, as did the Heileman Brewing Company. (Did you know there were a dozen brewing companies in Chicago back then? Me either. And they were not microbreweries either.) Sky Harbor Airport posted a trophy. The Chicago chapter of the National Aeronautics Association, headed by Jack Vilas, donated another trophy. (Vilas was the first man to fly across Lake Michigan in 1915.) The Standard Oil Company offered 250 gallons of seventy-two-octane fuel and 50 gallons of forty SAE oil. To show that not too much has changed in seventy years, except the prices, the organizers had to shell out $136 for liability insurance and $20 more for rain insurance.

Left: Harlem Airport Civil Air Patrol member Loretta Bennett (Sincora), 1950s. *Bob Zilinsky.*

Below: Fred and Eleanor Schumaker of Harlem Airport. *Craig Mantegna.*

Another good fellow volunteered to set up five loud speakers and a 110-volt generator at the south end of the field where the cars were to be parked. They were not going to charge admission, but twenty-five cents a car might cover their costs, they thought. The day of the show, September 25, arrived with perfect weather. There had been daily showers for the past three weeks, but now the field was dry. Ten county highway policemen and four state troopers arrived. The county cops were going to help on the field, while the troopers would keep the highway clear. For some reason, the troopers kept the traffic moving right past the airport and into the Stop N Sock golf driving range on the west side of Harlem. They were charging fifty cents per car and had room for about 3,000 cars. The airport could hold only 1,500 after the troopers finally let them on the field. Although little consolation, it was later discovered that the guy collecting the money for the golf range ran off with $1,200 of the $1,500 collected.

The show began with a three-ship formation fly-over by some of the boys from "Shoe's" school. There were fifty light planes on the field lined up so the crowd could get a good look at them. Twenty or so larger planes were also on the field. The roads within three miles were packed with an estimated fifteen thousand people. The county cops on the field apparently were not up to the job. The crowd ignored the cops and the temporary fences and rushed onto the field. The senior CAA inspector blew his top. He shut down everything until the field was cleared. In addition, he took a red pencil to some of the acts he felt were dangerous, even though they had been previously approved by the junior inspectors. These were the paper-cutting contest and the landing-over-a-barrier contest. The barrier was to be a string with balloons attached. If a plane hit the barrier, no damage would have resulted, and the pilots were all commercially rated. The paper-cutting contest was a feature at many air shows of the day. A streamer or a roll of toilet paper was pitched overboard at about four or five thousand feet, and the contestant dove to see how many times he could cut it with the propeller before it hit the ground.

But the act that almost caused the inspector heart failure was put on by Dave Bishop. Described as a crazy flying act, many skillful pilots put on a display of low-altitude aerobatics, as they are called now, disguised as drunks, hayseed farmers, little old schoolteachers or whatever, who somehow managed to steal an airplane that was conveniently left with the engine running. Sometimes, the show's announcer, who of course was in on the act, would tell the crowd someone's grandma was going up for her first airplane ride. The pilot would get out, inspecting a stuck tail wheel or something, and Granny, who was a pilot in disguise, would open the throttle—accidentally, of course—and the show was on. The announcer worked the crowd for all it was worth until the spectators caught on. Bishop became a pilot in the Air Transport Command during World War II and operated a charter and freight air service out of Midway Airport in the 1960s. He came to a tragic end departing Meigs Field one winter day when both engines failed. He survived the ditching but not the icy waters of Lake Michigan.

Other acts were precision-landing contests from 180-degree and 360-degree overhead approaches and bomb dropping with paper bags of flour. Two parachutists concluded the show with what was supposed to be a delayed fall from ten thousand to three thousand feet. Both had jumped previously but apparently got their signals mixed up and pulled their ripcords too early. A strong southwest wind aloft blew them east of the Municipal Airport, and one of them almost collided with an airliner. Chauncey Spencer was one of the jumpers and might have been the only African American airman in the show. Although not an actual Tuskegee Airman, he was one of the framers of the organization.

The organizers of the show, which included Wayne Thomis, aviation editor of the *Chicago Tribune*, learned a lot about how not to put on an air show. When all the income was totaled up from the parking fees and concessionaires, and they had paid their expenses, they had nine dollars leftover. They must have had a good time, however, because they decided to do it again the next year. But the world had changed by September 1939. Harlem Airport survived until the mid-1950s, and this is just one of the many stories born there.

The lyrics of a popular song of the prewar era by Ella May Morse describe the atmosphere at the time:

> *Blitzkrieg Baby, you can't bomb me; cause I'm pleadin' neutrality,*
> *Got my gun out, don't you see, Blitzkrieg Baby, you can't bomb me.*
> *Blitzkrieg Baby, you look so cute, all dressed up in your parachute,*
> *Let that Propaganda be, Blitzkrieg Baby you can't bomb me*

The above story is based on an article by Kurt Rand in Popular Aviation *magazine, December 1938.*

HINSDALE AIRPORT

With apologies to Nat "King" Cole, it was possible at one time to "Get Your Flips on Route 66." This was because at one time there were four small airports along that celebrated highway within fifty miles of Chicago. Stinson Field was located a few miles west of Municipal (Midway) Airport, across the Illinois River and canal on Fifty-fifth Street and Route 66. That airport and even the famous road are now part of a huge gravel pit. Lewis, which began as the Lewis Holy Name School of Aeronautics in Lockport, is now a regional reliever airport. And Wilhemi, south of Joliet, was known as the Joliet Airport until the Municipal Airport was built by the WPA (Works Progress Administration) in the 1930s. Route 66 is now known as Route 53 next to these last two. But the subject of this historical piece was back up the road (a piece), adjacent to what are now the Stevenson Expressway, I-55 and the Kingery Expressway, Route 83.

The Hinsdale Airport was actually three miles south of Hinsdale, population about 3,500 in the early 1940s, when Charles Feris started developing the 180-acre field, but it was common practice to name an airport for the closest town or village. Other than farmland, the only other features on the landscape were Ruth Lake, the country club at Sixty-third Street, the Hinsdale Pet Cemetery along Madison Avenue and, of course, the soon-to-be-historic Route 66.

Born in 1911, Feris started flying at the age of fourteen, even before the boom in aviation began with Charles Lindbergh spanning the Atlantic solo in 1927. It was said Feris was later a pilot for both Pan American and TWA

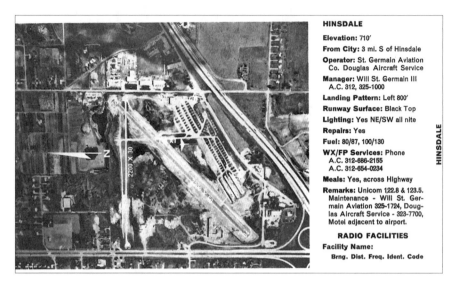

HINSDALE

Elevation: 710'

From City: 3 mi. S of Hinsdale

Operator: St. Germain Aviation Co. Douglas Aircraft Service

Manager: Will St. Germain III A.C. 312, 325-1000

Landing Pattern: Left 800'

Runway Surface: Black Top

Lighting: Yes NE/SW all nite

Repairs: Yes

Fuel: 80/87, 100/130

WX/FP Services: Phone A.C. 312-686-2155 A.C. 312-654-0234

Meals: Yes, across Highway

Remarks: Unicom 122.8 & 123.5. Maintenance - Will St. Germain Aviation 325-1724, Douglas Aircraft Service - 323-7700, Motel adjacent to airport.

RADIO FACILITIES

Facility Name:

Brng. Dist. Freq. Ident. Code

Hinsdale Airport, 1971. *Illinois Airport Directory.*

(at that time, Transcontinental and Western Airline). But I would imagine he didn't fit into the mold of an airline pilot. Shortly after opening the airport, he joined the war effort by becoming a test pilot at the Willow Run Factory in Detroit, where they were turning out B-24 bombers by the thousands. He was most likely a production test pilot, someone who routinely flew the planes as they came off the production line to see if everything was working properly. This is in contrast to the Clark Gable types depicted in movies of the 1930s who dove the super new fighter planes to see if the wings would stay on. But I would imagine that production test pilots had a few interesting flights that broke up the routine as well.

The first time I landed on Hinsdale was in the summer of 1965. My wife and I had just purchased our first airplane, an Aeronca L-3B, ex–army liaison and artillery spotter, from Frank Ament at Sandwich Airport and were seeking a place to tie it down. I parked near the gas pump and went looking for the man in charge but found no one except two guys watching the ballgame on TV. When I returned to the ship, I found it pushed back into the weeds. A very disagreeable fellow told me to "get the hell off his airport and never come back!" I tried to tell him I wanted to rent a tie down, but to no avail. So we moved the ship to Joliet Airport, where two months later it was flipped over three times in a tornado. All things have a deeper meaning, I have discovered. Events have a way of evening out.

Perhaps what made Feris so ill tempered was all the clearing, leveling and grading he had to do to make his land halfway decent as an airport. If the 1954 *Illinois Airport Directory* diagram of the field is any gauge of the condition of the land, he had quite a job on his hands. Two turf runways formed a *T*. The chart notes a hill ten feet high at the southwest corner, another hill thirty feet high at the northwest corner and a "rough area, rocks and stones," at the south end of the north–south runway. There were restrooms, fuel, service and storage available—even meals. The telephone number was 2795. Altogether, it was not much better or worse than some other fields in the area. But one great attraction was its location, on the heavily traveled Route 66.

Long before Feris bought the land, a small gas station and lunch counter started up at the corner of Madison Avenue and Route 66. Two local farm women struck a deal with the lunch counter owner, Irv Kolarik. If he would buy their chickens, they would teach him their recipe for fried chicken. He did, and they did and with all the traffic on Route 66, the two-car repair bay was soon turned into a restaurant. The Chicken Basket, as it became known, came about in 1946 and is one of the remaining features of area. It became a stop for the Blue Bird bus line, which ran from Chicago to Los Angeles on Route 66. The floorshow while you enjoyed your dinner was watching the little airplanes come and go. Some of these patrons were members of a flying club called Suburban Aviation. This club, formed in the 1950s, often ended a day of aviating at the Chicken Basket. Remnants of the club still meet occasionally, doing the next best thing to actually flying: "hangar flying."

Charles Mettler, a pilot at Hinsdale in December 1945 and later with United Airlines, had a tragic experience. A thirty-three-year-old woman from Joliet purchased a short sightseeing flight and somehow managed to undo her seatbelt and open the cabin door. Before Mettler could stop her, she left the airplane. All he could do was grab one of her shoes. All this happened above the Hinsdale High School football field. The *Chicago Tribune* of December 23, 1945, reported that the woman, Mrs. Louise Austin Scott, had attempted the same thing at the Joliet Airport three weeks earlier but had not succeeded.

In 1960, the land to the west and north of the airport was incorporated and became Willow Brook. In 1967, Feris and his wife, Dorothy, sold the airport. They had purchased the bankrupt Taylorcraft Aviation Corporation two years earlier and needed funds to sustain the manufacturing of the two-place high-wing monoplane. C.G. Taylor was a brilliant aircraft designer and had actually designed the world-famous Piper Cub. His business ability did not match his engineering skills, however, and he left Piper Aircraft and started his own company prior to World War II. His T-craft was twenty miles per hour faster than the Cub on the same horsepower but did not survive the postwar sales slump.

The new owners of the airport were William and Wilma St. Germain. They had been tenants on the field since 1958 and had built their training and sales operation into one of the major aviation centers in the Chicago area. They operated thirty aircraft, taught two-hundred-plus students and ran one of the largest Piper dealerships.

Feris stayed on as manager and saw to the improvement of the airport. The north–south runway was closed, and a 3,200-foot diagonal northeast-southwest runway was laid out. Land along Route 83 was leased for the construction of a Holiday Inn. In 1971, Will St. Germain contracted cancer and shortly thereafter succumbed to it. One of St. Germain's flight instructors, Lawrence "Dutch" Morrison, managed the field until Wilma St. Germain sold the property in 1973. It was rumored that the Holiday Inn people wanted to keep the runway, but the land became too valuable. Willow Brook annexed the field, and it became the industrial park it is today. It all came about quite suddenly, it seemed to me. I was commuting to Midway Airport daily in our second airplane, a 1948 Stinson Station Wagon, when I noticed the X on the runway ends one evening on the way home.

But this was not the end of the airport entirely. You might have noticed a large helicopter lifting big air-conditioning units on to some big plant or warehouse. Chances are, it belonged to Midwest Helicopter Airways, which began operations at Hinsdale in 1968 in the only hangar left on the field along Madison Avenue. Also, every six months or so, a group called the Midway Historians meets at an Irish pub across the road from the Chicken Basket restaurant. So it just goes to show, an airport might be gone but not entirely forgotten.

Recently, at a dinner meeting of some of the few remaining members of the Suburban Aviation Club, I met one of the charter members of the club, Charles "Chuck" Doose. Chuck told me he was the first man to land at Hinsdale when it first opened after the war. He was flying a forty-horsepower Taylorcraft at the time, and his was also the last plane, a Piper twin Comanche, out of the field when it closed. As a young fellow in 1940, Chuck said he would ride the Douglas Park elevated train to Mannheim Road and then walk, carrying a mop and a bucket, to the Westchester Airport at Roosevelt and Wolf Roads. (Quite a hike!) There he would wash airplanes in exchange for flying time. (Those sod and unpaved airports were notoriously muddy.) This is where he probably first met Charles Feris, who was the manager of the field at one time. An example of Chuck's feistiness was related to me by his son. Apparently, Chuck was trying to determine the source of an oil leak in the engine compartment of his T-craft one day. With the engine running, he gingerly lifted the cowling and peered inside, but his arm got a little too close to the propeller. In spite of the gash inflicted, he drove himself to the hospital emergency room and survived to fly another day.

There are most likely many more stories waiting to be told, probably one for every pilot who ever flew from that bumpy field, in spite of the cranky old guy who chased me away. I'll keep my ears open.

LANSING MUNICIPAL AIRPORT

Like a few other airports in the Chicago area, Lansing does not really qualify as a lost airport because it still exists, but in a highly altered state. The same can be said for Pal-Waukee (Executive now), Du Page, Waukegan and Joliet. They all had their beginnings some eighty years ago but were fortunate to survive the growth of suburbia and therefore contain a wealth of history and stories that should not be allowed to disappear.

It is a little-known fact even to the aviation community that Lansing was built by Henry Ford and his son Edsel in 1927. It's a shame that Edsel, who did so much to advance early aviation, is probably only known today as the namesake of the ugliest automobile of the 1960s. (Some say the grill of the 1959 Edsel looked like it was sucking a lemon.) The airfield was needed to support the Ford factory at nearby Hegeswisch. Ford purchased 1,400 acres of farmland next to the Illinois state line, extending into Munster, Indiana. The original hangar, which was designed by noted architect Albert Kahn, still stands on the northwest corner of the field at the intersection of Glenwood-Lansing Road and Burnham Avenue. It was placed on the National Register of Historic Places in 1985. On the west side of the hangar was a small waiting room, probably the first airport passenger terminal. It resembled the railroad waiting rooms of the era—but smaller, of course. By contrast, the Chicago Municipal Airport terminal was a muddy wooden shack until an up-to-date terminal was built in 1931.

Between the hangar and the intersection is a restored Bell HU-1 "Huey" helicopter honoring the veterans of the Vietnam War. You might

Carl "Breezy" Unger at Lansing Airport, 2010. *Selig*

say Lansing Airport spans fifty years of history right there in that corner of the field.

The extent to which the Fords advanced the airline industry is another obscure piece of history. Their involvement goes far beyond the corrugated metal tri-motor transports they produced and which led the industry out of the wood and fabric biplane era. The development of the radio navigational beacon by Ford engineers in conjunction with the Bureau of Standards and the U.S. Air Service allowed the fledging airline industry to begin flying through the weather instead of hedge-hopping under it. The first such radio beacon in Illinois was installed at the Lansing Airport, while at about the same time a young airmail pilot named Lindbergh was still scud-running into the airmail field at Maywood (when he wasn't taking to his parachute, that is). Lansing became the western end of the Ford Air Transportation Service, the first regularly scheduled commercial airline in the country, which connected the Detroit Dearborn plant with the Cleveland plant at the eastern end of the airway. This experimental air service continued until 1932, when Ford felt it had demonstrated the feasibility of commercial aviation and all operating and cost information was freely shared with the newly emerging airlines.

It is interesting to note that the birth of the Ford Motor Company and the Wright brothers' first powered flight occurred in the same year: 1903.

When Glenn Curtiss was nearly put out of business fighting the Wright brothers' patent lawsuits, Henry Ford comforted Curtiss by reminding him that he, Ford, had gone through the same trouble with patents concerning the first automobiles.

During the 1930s, the airport became known as the Chicago-Hammond Airport. Ford sold it in 1937. By then, the field was about 165 acres of sod. It was an "all-way field," as they were called then, with no definite runways. Landings and takeoffs could be made in whatever direction the wind blew. In winter, the planes were put on skis. This was common practice at sod fields as it was impractical to plow.

A very determined young lady, Virginia Rabung, was one of the many who flew out of Lansing on skis. She started her flying career at Rubinkam Airport in Markham and then at Stinson Airport in McCook, Illinois, in 1943. Living on the North Side of Chicago, this involved a bus ride into the city and a second bus ride on Route 66 to the airport since she didn't know how to drive and had no car. These small airports were not set up to handle girls in those days, and it took a lot of courage to face the superior-male attitude that prevailed. After soloing, she found companionship at a dinner at the Chicago Girls Flying Club (organized by Mae Wilson at her airfield on Lawrence Avenue and River Road before the war). She won a raffle at the dinner entitling her to a free hour of flying time at Lansing. After another long bus ride and a mile walk, she made her first cross-country flight from there prior to obtaining her private pilot license. Virginia went on to many flying adventures, including a flight to Cuba in her Cessna 140. She self-published a book in 2009 entitled *Virginia, Where Do You Keep the Parachute?*

As mentioned elsewhere, Lansing, like many other flying fields during World War II, was utilized under the Civilian Pilot Training Program. Various colleges in the Chicago area conducted the ground school classes leading to private pilot licenses while the students were bused to the fields for flight training. While some of the newly minted pilots were able to meet the higher medical standards of the military flight schools (baseball great Ted Williams, for example), the majority became flight instructors after completing advanced courses in aerobatics and obtaining commercial licenses. Many remained in that occupation for the duration of the war, but the burnout rate caused some to join the Ferry Command, moving aircraft from factories to bases across the country. Still others became part of the Air Transport Command, moving aircraft and supplies around the world. The most notable of this command, in my mind, are the pilots who flew "the Hump" in the CBI (China-Burma-India) theater of operations. See if you can find a copy of *Flying the Hump* by Jeff Ethell and Don Downie, published by Motorbooks International, MBI Publishing, in 2002.

The first time Suzette and I set foot on Lansing was in the 1960s. It was still a sod field but had the grass mowed for several runways. Southtown Aviation Corporation was the operator, and Eleanor Schumacher was the manager. Wilbur Bole of Cruiser Airways was her partner, I believe, after husband, Fred, died. They had operated at Harlem Airport for many years until it, too, became suburbia. There was a big Quonset hangar and a few wooden buildings in addition to the Ford hangar. I believe an engine shop, G&N, was there. That spring of 1965 had been quite rainy, and the whole field was a lake. Takeoffs and landings were made on the gravel ramp. What brought us out to this far southern field was a fellow I worked with at Midway Airport, Carl Unger. He offered to let us fly his new home-built airplane, the "Breezy," a plane you rode "on" not "in." Sue and I are probably the only people who have not flown the Breezy. We firmly insist on having something up around our shoulders when we fly.

Suzette and I dropped into Lansing many times over the years, visiting Carl and attending EAA Chapter 261 fly-in breakfasts. Before the present management took away the airport courtesy car, we were able to stock up at a to-die-for bakery in Calumet near 186th Street and a great farm stand on Glenwood-Lansing Road west of the airport. For many years, Shannon's Landing on the second floor of the administration building was a good lunch stop, even if we aviators were unable to partake of its adult beverages. Until recently, a group of aging aviators who called themselves the "Lunchwaffe" would meet and fly off to some airport for lunch. We always enjoyed visiting with Bob Malkas, airport manager from the mid-1980s into the first decade of the twenty-first century, who, although not a pilot, had much to do with making the airport what it is today.

Near the end of World War II, the government began selling more than twelve thousand surplus aircraft at twenty various airfields across the country. Fifty such aircraft, ranging from Aeroncas ($375) to Stinson Relients ($6,700), were available at Ford-Lansing, as it was called then. An article in the November 1946 issue of *Flying* magazine tells a very interesting story of two girls who toured the country in an Aeronca L-3B, possibly purchased right there at Lansing. Dorothy "Gypsy" Nichols, a graduate of Merrillville, Indiana high school, grew up on a chicken farm in Crown Point, Indiana, and learned to fly at Lansing in November 1944. Her flight instructor was Fred O. Perkins, an AAF veteran. Her parents were so against flying that they talked her brothers into the walking army, navy and marines, but she learned to fly on the sly. She and her girlfriend, Frances Horn, from Gary, Indiana, traveled the South and Southwest in the Aeronca, something like the gypsy flyers of a previous age. They worked as waitresses and short-order cooks to finance the trip and found many new friends when they got lost and/or ran out of gas and landed in farm fields or on ranches. When they landed next to a school in Texas, the school was let out for the day. Another time, they delivered plasma for the Red Cross to the victims of a hurricane. In all, they traveled twenty thousand miles at eighty miles per hour, about 250 hours flying time, when gasoline was twenty-five cents a gallon.

I have not been able to trace these two adventurers through the Lansing Historical Society, but I bet that would make another interesting story. It's just another example of what happens when a person catches a dose of "aviation."

LEARNING TO FLY—
FOR REAL

And the music goes down and around and comes out here.
—Jimmy and Tommy Dorsey and the Clambake Seven, 1940

There's an old saying that goes, "When you become a teacher, from your students you shall learn." Something like that. It's probably supposed to rhyme, too. But regardless, as true as it turned out to be, that was the farthest thing from my mind when I decided to become a flight instructor. I just wanted to fly and get paid for it. A bum right eye ruled out the airlines. I had used up the benefits from the GI Bill I had earned defending the country from the threat of Communism during the Cold War (which lasted for another thirty-five years). Thanks to the employee discount allowed by Priester Aviation Services at Pal-Waukee Airport, I completed training and earned a commercial license, multi-engine and instrument rating. This allowed me to begin flying charter trips in the C-182, the Bonanzas, a Piper Apache and an occasional gig as copilot on a Beech 18. It was very educational transporting businessmen to the various cities and states in the Midwest in the early 1960s. It was a bit of a different world then.

My multi-engine training was in a Piper PA-23 Apache N27V. I might be wrong, but someone once told me this airplane was two wrecks put together as one. If so, the guys in the shop did an excellent job. It flew great. I had left Priester the previous winter for a job in Muskegon, Michigan, where I discovered it snowed all the time! Many exciting adventures were had that winter, and when I am sure the statute of limitations has expired, I might

Pal-Waukee Airport, 1958. *Ted Koston.*

write about them. Back at Pal-Waukee, exciting things began to occur. I have always said that my favorite airplane is whichever one I was flying at the time, but 27V was a sweet flying machine. Sitting tall between two motors was intoxicating for a guy who started out in a J-3 Cub. After about twenty hours dual, Charlie Priester signed me off for a check ride, and I hastened over to the Du Page FAA office in June 1961.

The inspector I rode with was a very good flyer. Most of the FAA people of that era were ex–World War II guys who really knew their stuff. Mr. Kurtts was a big man and entirely bald. He was known as "Mr. Clean" (but not to his face) because he resembled a well-known TV commercial character. Inspectors were not supposed to do any teaching, just pass or fail, but the good ones couldn't help themselves. Mr. Clean noticed right off my reluctance to bank too steeply into the dead engine. So he had me do steep 720-degree turns that way until I realized the ship was not going to fall out of the sky. He also told me it was better to climb out after takeoff at the best angle of climb in order to have plenty of altitude if an engine quit. I had been climbing out flatter at higher air speed. (This is still one of those barroom arguments.) So, after he passed me, I was so elated and impressed with the performance of a steep climb at minimum weight, I forgot to raise the landing gear! I flew all the way back to Pal-Waukee with the gear hanging out and didn't notice a thing wrong until I went to lower it.

We had just resurrected a World War II Stearman biplane, N5404N, in the shop, and it joined the Priester fleet in the spring of 1961. (George Priester had flown a Stagger Wing Beechcraft N5400N some years earlier with John Cameron Swayze, a well-known newsman of the era and later a pitch man for a watch company. Remember, "It takes a licking and keeps on ticking." It was called the "Camel News Caravan.") The Stearman rented for the same rate as the Cubs—twelve dollars dual and eight solo. I could not pass up this chance to fly a real "war bird," although this term had not been invented yet. It was just another war-surplus airplane, although it was a bit different from all the Stearmans I was to come across later. It had a two-piece sliding canopy, for one thing. Apparently, it had been used to train Canadian pilots. During my spin training, Jack Layer and I discovered that the canopy rattled like crazy, and during spins to the right, it made a loud thud. Since it was still summer, the canopy was removed. It had a Lycoming 225-horsepower seven-cylinder engine with the exhaust manifold in front of the crankcase instead of the usual Continental engine. Also, there was no electrical system, so it had to be propped like a Cub. Jack Layer and I did numerous spins, lazy eights, pylon and "on eights," 1,080-degree overhead approaches, chandelles and wheel landings until they were coming out of my ears. I had never had so much fun! So, in late August 1961, back I went to Du Page in the Stearman, this time, to become (drum roll!) a flight instructor.

But it was not to be. Another very nice guy, Inspector Marshall Balfe, rode with me on a nice day, and it was a nice ride until the last wheel landing on the short runway, runway four, which is a taxiway now. I had touched down light as a feather and was rolling along tail high when a puff of wind barely kissed the tail and started us off toward the tall grass. When my foot went for the rudder pedal to correct, it wasn't there. Mr. Balfe had already stomped his pedal in the back pit and taken control—an automatic failure. Of course, in another second, I would have saved the day. It served me right. I had underestimated Mr. Balfe. I had been wearing a backpack chute in the front pit, and he wore a seat pack chute in back. When I looked in the mirror as we taxied out, I saw he was sitting so high that his chin was about level with the top of the windshield. I thought, "This guy can't be too swift if he can't figure out how to adjust the seat." And when we did the two turn spins, I thought for sure he would fall out of the airplane. But he gave me an incomplete instead of a failure. Jack tried to make me feel better by telling me that they always failed about 75 percent of instructor applicants on the first ride. I went back a week later after five hours' more time and passed. And again I learned something. Mr. Kurtts, who rode with me the second time, informed me that we were not flying a Stearman but a Boeing B-75N1. He could have told me it was a Curtiss Condor and I would have believed him, as long as he passed me.

So I became a limited flight instructor (LFI). Many people have thought me "limited" in many ways, but this was the first time I had received official recognition. Actually, I thought the LFI rating was a good idea, and why it didn't last much longer I'll never know. What it meant was that a new instructor had to serve an apprenticeship, more or less, under an experienced instructor. His first five pre-solo students had to be checked by a senior instructor before they were allowed to solo. Only then, if they passed, would the LFI become a fully certificated CFI. Personally, when they did away with this idea, I thought this was the beginning of the blind really leading the blind—and the start of an inbreeding of instructors, which continues to this day. But don't get me started.

One day, I was standing in front of the brick hangar when I saw the Stearman (I mean Boeing) taxiing across the ramp with a girl's little head bobbing from side to side trying to see around the big radial engine. She was a cute little thing wearing a white cloth helmet, and I thought, "What's that little chick doing in that great big airplane?" A peculiarity of this Boeing was sticky brakes. Just the lightest touch of the brake pedal would pop the tail up about two inches. As she taxied by, S turning as was necessary to see around the nose, the airplane appeared to be hiccupping whenever she tapped the brakes. She later became an instructor as well. But that's another story with a very happy ending.

Sadly, the Boeing did not come to a happy ending. The ailerons on these planes were on ball bearings, and the slightest breeze would bang the control stick back and forth if left unlocked. The locking mechanism was designed for military people and was a bit complicated. One sunny fall afternoon, a fellow took his girl for a ride and ended up stalled out over an apple orchard north of the field. They were just high enough to make about a half turn of a spin. The ship went straight nose-down into the trees. The wood wings shredded as they went through the branches, and by the time the ship hit the ground, it was at a standstill. The pilot and his girl stepped to the ground a little dazed but completely unharmed.

I enjoyed flying with what I called "retreads," the veterans of World War II. Even after twenty-year layoffs, their stick and rudder skills came right back to them—especially the navy-trained ones. They were in their forties then, which seemed old to me, and with their families raised, they could now afford to fly again. A couple fellows were sharp except for crosswind landings, and I couldn't figure out why until one explained. He had flown four-engine flying boats, and they always landed into the wind. The other flew off a carrier. They also headed into the wind for most operations. By contrast, I was asked to give a quick checkout to a young USAF pilot so he could take his girl for a Sunday afternoon ride in a 172. This fellow had flown three different airplanes during his training. A T-28, a B-25 and a B-47 jet bomber. He attempted our first takeoff with his feet flat on the floor, control wheel firmly gripped in his gloved hands. So much for a quick checkout! I hope I was tactful, but I was pretty green myself.

Although an instructor could lose some weight in the winter, he could make it up in the summer and then some. We were paid only for flying time, no salary. Having an A&P ticket, I could help out in the shop in slow months. But in the summer, we often flew from sunup to sundown. So quick checkouts between scheduled students or at lunchtime were a common occurrence. One standard procedure scares me to think about now. In fact, not knowing the statute of limitations on such antics, perhaps I recall only hearing of such things during some long-ago hangar-flying sessions. Sally's gang, Art Teske, Joe Flotter or George Group might have been the guilty parties. But "someone" determined that the quickest way to do a fast checkout in a J-3 was to let the student take it around the pattern and then, on short final, tell him to follow closely on the controls. The CFI would flare out as if to make a wheel landing, but then a quick push of the stick would bounce the ship twenty feet or so. Then the CFI would hold up his hands and shout, "You've got it!" If the "checkee" poured the coal to it and went around, fine. If he added power and recovered in the remaining runway, better yet. He got signed off OK for solo, and the CFI got to finish his lunch. For a fast checkout in one of the Cessnas, a full-flap go-around with normal nose-up trim for landing usually told the tale. For years, Cessnas had forty degrees of flap operated manually with a big lever between the seats. The L-19 "Bird Dog" had sixty degrees! Sometime in the late 1970s, the FAA, in its infinite wisdom, deemed this unsafe. Later, Cessnas were limited to thirty degrees of flap travel. Go figure.

One of the nicest young guys at Pal-Waukee at that time was Tommy Horaski, a good-looking high school kid. He worked for Sally's Flying Club as a line boy, probably in exchange for flying time. He and I were sharing some J-3 time one day and found ourselves over at Jack and Nancy Layer's house in Arlington Heights. We spotted Nancy in the backyard and cut the power and spiraled down, shouting her name. She looked left, right and all around but never up. Jack and Nancy and that sharp-looking little brunette in the Boeing and I would often have dinner at a Chinese place in the Heights called Chins. Nancy, a non-pilot, would be utterly bored with our airplane talk. She and her daughter were equestrians. I still picture Tommy in Chinos and penny loafers wiping down the belly of one of Sally's Cubs. He had bum eyesight but became a corporate and freighter pilot, at one time flying a giant of an airplane, a Curtiss C-46 Commando. We were sad to hear many years later that he had died in the crash of a rescue helicopter.

In the mid-1960s, the J-3s were getting pretty tired. Three brand-new Champion Citabrias came on the line. These were merely beefed-up Aeronca Champs with ninety-horsepower continental engines and spiffy paint jobs. A version is still made today up in Wisconsin. But a problem arose. A few Champs came back from the practice area with wing rib tapes popped loose. People were trying to do "airbatics" without adequate training. Too bad— they were really nice airplanes.

It was not until many years later that I read Charles Lindbergh's book *We*, in which he describes what it takes to be a successful flight instructor. You have to let the student go as far as is safe before taking over control, he states, or he loses confidence and never learns from his near mistakes. In return, the instructor learns much more about his craft. An example of an instructor who had evidently learned his craft was Bill Campbell. He was the first and only black pilot I had ever seen at that time. It wasn't until much later that I learned about the Tuskegee Airmen or Cornelius Coffey. I was sitting in a Cub with a student waiting in line to take off when this other J-3 came bouncing down the runway with Campbell in the front seat turned almost completely around, facing his student and gesturing earnestly as if having a discussion over a cup of coffee. He later went to New York and opened his own school and also went into show business. To the other extreme, there was one instructor who followed his student so closely on the controls that when allowed to solo, the student had no idea why the airplane reacted so strangely and lost control. There is an old USAAF drinking song that ends with the words: "You can always tell a fighter pilot. But not much!" The same can be said for a new flight instructor.

I'm sure everyone has seen the movie *Brigadoon* with Gene Kelly about the village that only appears once every one hundred years. One of my students and I had a similar experience one day returning from a cross-country trip. Actually, we were just a little bit lost. I knew we were

Victory Air Museum, near Wauconda and Barrington. *Ted Koston.*

somewhere near Bangs Lake at Wauconda, Illinois, but otherwise we could see nothing but lakes and trees. This was before all the condos were built. I decided to give my student an emergency landing so the afternoon would not be an entire waste. I cut the power, and we spiraled down to an opening in the trees. When we had the field made, we started a go-around, and we were amazed to see some old World War II planes parked under the trees. It looked like an aerial junkyard. We circled a few times and saw more planes near a farmhouse. We were getting low on fuel and daylight, so we headed for home with the idea to return again someday. This is where the *Brigadoon* part comes in. I tried several times to find that farm again, but all in vain. After a while, I forgot about it. Fast-forward about forty years. I'm now an aero historian, amateur grade. My good friend Ted Koston, an aerial photographer of no little renown in the Chicago area, is showing me some of his collection of slide pictures. And what do you think comes up? An aerial shot of a farmhouse with World War II planes all around. It's near Wauconda, and it was called the Victory Air Museum. Our Brigadoon again, and it took only forty years, not one hundred, to reappear. Of course, it was long gone, along with its originators. The picture had been taken in 1969, about five years after my discovery with my student. There is more to this story, but I'll save it for another time.

By the end of the 1960s, a control tower was built at Pal-Waukee, the Cubs were replaced with tricycle-gear Cessna 150s with radios and it was the end of an era. I was very happy to have been part of it and of the new world of corporate and business aviation that Priester Aviation Services brought into being.

THE HAND OF GOD

In the early 1960s, the intersection of Route 59 and North Avenue, Route 64, was pretty much open fields and country. Driving out to Du Page County Airport to take a written examination (they were free then and done with number-two lead pencils, not computers) was a pretty long trip from my home in Elmwood Park on the outskirts of Chicago. But when I came upon that intersection, I knew I was close.

The only buildings there were on the northwest corner. A red brick building about two or three stories high stretched across the intersection diagonally, forming a triangle with the two highways. On the corner stood a statue of Christ with his arms outstretched to His sides, similar to the one on the mountaintop in Rio, Brazil. Except this one was in an enclosure with an arched top, facing southeast. I believe the building was a religious school or perhaps a monastery.

One Sunday afternoon, my buddy Rich Gearhart and I were returning from Joliet after visiting Rich's girl (and future wife), who was a student at St. Francis College. We had all grown up within blocks of one another in Elmwood Park at the end of the Grand Avenue streetcar line. Rich and I had been gas pump jockeys in high school. He worked evenings and weekends at a Shell station, while I did the same at a Phillips 66 station on Diversey Avenue. Kids today flip hamburgers, but we had many more options in the 1950s. We could stock shelves at the local A&P store, usher at the Elm Theater or jerk sodas at the drugstore—even caddy at the Oak Park Country Club. The land of opportunity, right?

Du Page County Airport, 1962. *Tim Coltrin.*

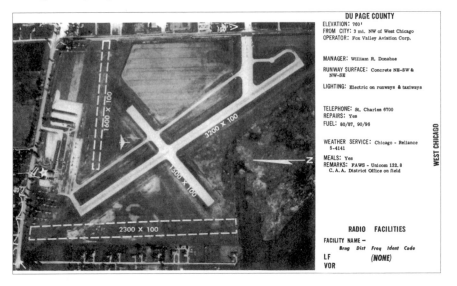

Du Page County Airport, 1954. *Illinois Airport Directory.*

Now Rich was climbing telephone poles for Ma Bell, and I was an airplane mechanic and a fairly new private pilot. I had rented an almost new Cessna 172, a straight-tail '56 model, from Priester Aviation Services at Pal-Waukee Airport, where I was employed.

We were about halfway back to Pal-Waukee when we encountered some snow showers. The wind must have shifted onshore from Lake Michigan. It went from clear and sunny but cold to a shower here and there. At that time, I knew nothing about weather off the lake. Thinking it was just a local thing, I dodged one shower after another. The clear spaces in between grew smaller and smaller. Pretty soon, all I knew was that we were somewhere between Joliet and Pal-Waukee. The showers became more numerous as we went on, and pretty soon the ground was only visible here and there. No landmarks could be seen, just farms and trees. I finally decided to turn around, and just as I dipped the left wing down, right below us was the statue of Jesus with his arms outstretched, as if saying, "It's OK, boys, I've got you." I knew immediately where we were, two miles east of Du Page County Airport. In fact, the statue's right arm was pointing right at the airport. We must have passed right next to the airport unseen in the snow showers. I turned and followed North Avenue west to the airport, made a very short approach and landed. Thankfully, this was prior to the control tower being built

While tying the airplane down for the night, my buddy Rich, in his best imitation of Oliver Hardy, said, "Here's another fine mess you've gotten me into." And I said, "Thank Jesus for getting us out of it!" The FBO (Fox Valley Aviation) was just closing up; it was dark now, but we were able to call Rich's brother for a long ride home and Pal-Waukee to report our RON (remain overnight). Rich flew with me for many years after that day. He probably thought I had learned a lesson, and I truly had. Actually, I had learned it years ago in Sunday school. A song we used to sing went: "Jesus loves me, this I know, for the Bible [statue] tells me so."

The monastery and statue are gone now, replaced by a mini-mart gas station. The fields and farms are now houses, mega-stores and franchise restaurants. But I'll never forget that statue. Rich never fails to remind me of it whenever he comes north from his Florida retirement home. Climbing telephone poles turned out to provide a better pension than turning wrenches on broken airplanes.

ODDS AND ENDS

When I peruse Bob Beyer's list of "Airports That Used to Be," I find a few that I still know nothing about. And the chances of finding anyone who does grows dimmer with every passing day. So I thought I would record what little I know about some of these fields before I grow dimmer myself. Bob and friends might have compiled this list after a hard day's flying while relaxing with some adult beverages, so any discrepancies I mention should not be taken as criticisms but just as a viewpoint twenty years later. Bob was quite a guy. He used to ride his bike out the old Toonerville Trolley bike path all the way to Sycamore from Elmhurst until he passed on in the late 1990s.

One entry on Bob's list that always intrigued me is the airfield in Stone Park he calls "Nor-Man." The name evidently comes from the intersection of North Avenue and Mannheim Road. When I was just a kid during World War II, my family used to travel North Avenue en route to my grandparents' farm in Villa Park. I remember my dad mentioning that the factory on the northeast corner of the intersection was manufacturing army tanks for the war effort. I think it was the International Harvester plant. But before the war, it evidently was a flying field. Someone once told me they also flew model airplanes there.

Topping Bob's list was "Ackers" at Grand Avenue and Wolf Road. I've shown this list to many groups of flying people, and no one has heard of it. This is in the general vicinity of Sky Haven, which Bob shows at Wolf Road and Franklin Avenue between Bensenville and Schiller Park. (As you drive

Right: Ted Koston and CAP Aeronca L-16 at Machesney Airport, Rockford, Illinois, 1950s. *Ted Koston.*

Below: Stave Rock State Park landing strip on an island in the Illinois River, Utica, Illinois. *Selig.*

up the Tri-State 294 toll road, you'll pass right over it). It must predate Sky Haven, which opened about 1939, as I doubt two fields would have operated so close together.

Number eight on Bob's list is also a mystery. He labeled it as Cook County field at I-88 and the Fox River. There were several Cook County airfields shown in a 1927 publication, but the Fox River is in Kane County. The field in that location was actually called Aurora Airways, which lasted until 1967. The Aurora Airport at Sugar Grove was started in 1960, so Aurora had two airports for a while.

Two airfields are mentioned that might have been used by Ed Heath, the originator of the kit-built airplane in the 1920s. One is located at Potter, Dempster Street and Northwest Highway, and the other is in Morten Grove at Dempster Street and Waukegan Road. Heath flew at many fields on the northwest side of Chicago and even as far as Lake Zurich, where he tested a floatplane. More info on this astonishing aviation pioneer can be found in *The Heath Story* by Chet Peek, published by Tree Peaks Publishing in 2003.

The northwest airfield sent me on a merry chase when Bob located it at Milwaukee Road and Central Avenue, which put it in the Jefferson Park area of Northwest Chicago. The nice people of the historical society in that area set me straight and even provided me with a Maine Township map, which showed the airfield at Central Road (rather than Avenue). It was up the road a piece on Milwaukee Road, across from the Ridgewood Cemetery. I had never heard of this field until I discovered that Dick Lloyd had taken his first flying lessons there as a teenager. Lloyd was the second operator of Sky Haven Airport, as mentioned elsewhere.

Ashburn field at Eighty-third and Cicero, home of the famous Laird race planes, as well as Checkerboard Field, the Maywood Hines Field and Chicago Municipal, have been well covered in many publications. But there are a few other fields that Suzette and I have visited that should not fade away without some mention.

A favorite of Suzette's was the Wagon Wheel Resort at Rockton, north of Rockford. Originally built in the 1930s, the landing strip was not put in until the 1950s. This beautiful resort featured a golf course, riding stables, a swimming pool and ice rink, two hundred rooms in the lodge, a bowling alley, a banquet hall, a theater, shops and a church. Many well-known names of the era stopped there, including Bob Hope, John Wayne, golfer Jack Nicklaus, racecar driver Bobby Allison and USA champion figure skater Janet Lynn.

Just up the river on the north side of Rockford was the original Rockford Airport, opened in 1927 by Fred Machesney, a pioneer barnstormer and motorcycle racer from Kewanee, Illinois. After almost starving to death during the Great Depression, Machesney trained over three thousand pilots in the Civilian Pilot Training Program and, later, on the GI Bill program. Suzette and I attended a 99s meeting there once in the early 1970s before it became a shopping center. Probably one of the most notable events occurring there was the first attempt to establish a northern air route to Europe via the great Circle Route in 1928 by a real pioneer named "Fish" Hassell in a Stinson Detroiter. Look that one up in a book called *Viking with Wings* by Colonel Bert R.J. Hassell.

1. Ackers
   Grand Ave. & Wolf Rd.

2. American
   Devon & River Rd.

3. Arlington Hts.
   Central & Kirchoff Rds.

4. Ashburn
   (Aero Club Field)
   Cicero Ave. & 85 th St.

5. Chicago Flying Club
   Irving Park & Cumberland

6. Chicago Heights
   Ashland Ave. & 203rd St.

7. Chicagoland
   Rt. 45 - Wheeling

8. Cook County
   I-88 - Fox River

9. Dixie
   (Rubinkam)
   Rt. 1 & 199th St.

10. DuPage Airport
    (Air Activities Airport)
    Rt. 64 & Rt. 18

11. Elgin
    I-90 - Fox River

12. Elmhurst East
    Rt. 20 & Rt. 83

13. Elmhurst West
    Rt. 20 & Church Rd.

14. Ford Lansing Airport
    (Lansing Municipal Airport)
    Lansing Rd. & Burnham Rd.

15. Gear
    So. of New Lenox Rd. -
    West edge of town

16. Glenview N.A.S.
    (Curtis Reynolds)
    Lake St. & Shermer Rd.

17. Governors
    Monee & Indianwood in
    Urban Hills

18. Harlem
    Harlem & 87th St.

19. Heath
    Potter Dempster N W Hwy.

20. Hinsdale
    I-55 & Rt. 83

21. Howell
    Rt. 83 & Cicero Ave.

22. Joliet Park Dist. Airport
    (Joliet Municipal Airport)
    Rt. 52 & Houbolt

23. Lewis University Airport
    (Holy Name Technical
    School Airport)
    Plainfield Rd. & Joliet Rd.

24. Libertyville
    Rt.137 & River Rd.

25. Lombard (York Twp.)
    Finley Rd. & Roosevelt Rd.

26. Maywood
    (Hines Field)
    1st Ave. & Cermak Rd.

27. Midway Airport
    (Chicago Municipal Airport)
    59th & Cicero

28. Mitchell
    Rt. 53 N. of Army Trail Rd.

29. Morton Grove
    Dempster St. & Waukegan Rd.

30. Northwest
    Milwaukee Ave. & Central Ave. Rd.

31. Park Ridge
    River Rd. & Touhy

32. Prosperi
    Oak Park Ave. & 187th St.

33. Ravenswood
    York Rd. & Touhy

34. Sandell
    Rt. 45 - So. of PKE Airport

35. Sky Harbor
    Dundee & Wheeling Rd.

36. Sky Haven
    Wolf Rd. & Franklin Ave.

37. Snyder
    (Seaplane)
    South of Navy Pier

38. Stinson
    I-55 & 55th St.

39. Stone Park
    (Nor-Man)
    Rt. 45 & North Ave.

40. Triangle
    Rt. 30 & Rt. 41

41. Washington Pk.
    Halsted St. & 187th

42. Westchester
    Roosevelt Rd. & Wolf Rd.

43. Wilson
    Lawrence Ave. & River Rd.

44. Wood Dale
    Rt. 83 & Thorndale Ave.

45. Yackley - Checkerboard
    (Hines Field)
    Roosevelt Rd. & 1st Ave.

Contact Bob Beyer with other
airport locations or any
corrections you might have
at: 708•834•7560.

Bob Beyer and Stan Tonkin's list of forgotten airports.

A "just for fun" airport that no longer exists was located along the Illinois River in the Ottawa area. Starved Rock State Park was built in the 1930s by the Civilian Conservation Corps at Utica. At one time, there was a grass airstrip on an island in the Illinois River just across from the park. Although closed in the winter months, originally a free boat and then, later, a cable car carried visiting flyers to the lodge for one dollar. The runway was 3,100 by 200 feet, with tall trees along the edges. With the wind under ten knots, it was advisable to land east and take off west. There was a windsock on the River

Locks east of the airpark. A bridge crossing the river to the west provided a challenge as well. In the spring, if the river was high, the field could get a little soft. The 1975–76 Illinois Aeronautical Chart showed another state park airstrip along the Kankakee River about five miles northwest of Kankakee. There were no facilities there, just a nice spot to picnic along the river. It was a bit short, however—only 2,200 feet with trees all around. If the grass had not been cut recently, it was a dicey thing.

Another "fun" airstrip was the Prairie Lake Hunt Club on the north side of the Illinois River near Marseilles. It had a 1,900-foot north–south grass strip down the middle of its eighteen-hole golf course. It was really a nine-hole course, but the second nine had different tee-off spots. For a while, there was a range for shooting clay pigeons, too. At the north end was a large pond. One of the members of the Suburban Flying Club lost his Cessna 182 in the drink some years ago due to bad brakes. It wasn't badly damaged until someone tried to retrieve it by wrapping a steel cable around its aluminum fuselage. At the south end of the strip was a nice opening in the tree line big enough to fly through safely. At one time, the banquet room served a delicious German dinner on Sunday afternoons. A small train ran around the perimeter of the room near the ceiling. The golfers and the flyers got along quite well for the most part. Occasionally, a golfer would slice or hook a ball onto the runway, and a plane might have to go around, but I never heard of any accidents. Unfortunately, the lodge changed owners several times, and the last and most recent owner decided the liability was too expensive and planted trees down the runway.

Still another neat place to fly for lunch was the Marina at Seneca, also on the Illinois River. This was probably as close to "mountain flying" as any of us Midwest flatlanders would ever get. The paved runway was roughly north–south on the south side of the river, with rising terrain to the south that was wooded and hid a line of electrical wires. At that point, the river was about two hundred feet below the farmland on either side. Taking off north, you could turn and follow the river while gaining altitude. But going south, you had to be able to out-climb the terrain or else! Another couple in the Suburban Flying Club experienced the results of such a situation. The wind was no help down in the river valley and could be felt only if it was roaring out of the east or west. The owners of the marina extended the runway several times, every time they bought a bigger airplane. It was quite nice to eat lunch on the patio deck or inside the picture-window dining room and watch the boats come and go. They had a very large storage area for the boats in winter with a large mobile hoist. The indoor display room had boats of many sizes, and we were amazed that some of them cost less than our airplanes. Eventually, the owners became aware of the liability problem and no longer welcomed flyers. During the flood of 1997, I believe, the entire marina was under water.

Also noted on Beyer's list was Sandell Airport on Route 45, Milwaukee Road, just south of Pal-Waukee Airport. This was also shown on a 1935 Shell Oil Company road map, which placed it on Camp McDonald Road east of Wolf Road. Both of these roads were gravel at the time. Someone once mentioned that they thought the fellow who built the Rose Parakeet, a beautiful little aerobatic open-cockpit biplane, did so there, but I haven't been able to uncover anything about it. Could it have been Bill Rose of the meatpacking company in Barrington?

Bill Rose held some of the biggest and most well-attended fly-ins at his Wind Rose Farm in Barrington and, later, at his Compass Rose Farm near Marengo. It began as a free fly-in lunch for members of the Midwest Antique Aircraft Club and the Vintage Airplane Club only, but every year more people flew in, and Bill never turned anyone away. Finally, it became too large for even Bill to handle. He had a terrific collection of antique and classic airplanes, which numbered so many that he had a difficult time rounding up pilots to fly them all up to Oshkosh every summer.

Every now and then, someone asks me about an airfield in Evanston. Until lately, I had to confess ignorance (of which many people accuse me quite often). But recently, someone sent me a remarkable story of not an airfield, really, but merely an airstrip that was scraped out and leveled along the north branch of the Chicago River between Church and Dempster Streets. The story was written by Janet G. Messenger, a noted Evanston historian. The airstrip existed for only a short time during the 1950s, and although similar strips might have been built in other parts of the country, it is the only one known in the Chicago area. It was a product of the Cold War, when some people were building bomb shelters in their backyards in the event of a nuclear attack by our former allies, the Soviet Union.

The Red Cross, Evanston and St. Francis Hospitals, the Civil Air Patrol and the civil defense programs of Evanston and Skokie all participated in exercises to bring medical supplies and doctors to local hospitals and to carry victims to other cities. Thus, it was a civil defense airfield built in 1953 to provide aid to North Shore communities in the event of nuclear attack on Chicago. The strip was only 1,700 feet long by 75 feet wide and was marked with white gravel crosses at each end to show it was an emergency strip only. A well-attended dedication ceremony was held in May 1954, and the commander of Glenview Naval Air Station, Rear Admiral Daniel V. Gallery, addressed the crowd at the Evanston Township High School.

The first practice mission was run in July 1954 by ten CAP planes from Pal-Waukee, bringing in emergency supplies for the local hospitals. Some of the planes were piloted by Omar Dockstader, Charles Erickson, Reid Mathews and John Gans. But by the early 1960s, there was no longer a need for such preparedness, and the dirt strip became what it is today—a landscaped park for bikers, joggers, skaters and walkers. But perhaps the most interesting aspect, at least to this amateur historian, is the name of this forgotten airstrip: Eadie Field. Lieutenant William F. Eadie was a graduate of Evanston Township High School and a naval aviator serving in the Pacific during World War II. It was his scout floatplane that spotted the survivors of a B-17 bomber who had ditched in the ocean three weeks previously. The men in the raft were near death, and rather than wait for another ship or plane, Eadie loaded them on the wings of his plane and taxied to the nearest base forty miles away. This story can be read in the biography of Eddie Rickenbacker, who was a passenger on the B-17. The highlight of the Evanston Fourth of July celebration in 1943 was a mass flyover by Lieutenant Eadie and a formation of planes from Glenview. However, William Eadie did not survive the war. I certainly hope some plaque or monument marks the site of the former Eadie airstrip.

One Sunday afternoon shortly after the turn of the century, Suzette and I attended the annual Corn Fest Fly-In at Rochelle, Illinois. They served delicious pork sandwiches and sweet corn. But the greatest discovery of that day was a lady, Heather Marks, selling little paperback books at one of the display tables. The book, *The Eakle Family of Progress Corner*, was written by John Eakle, Heather's uncle, who became a P-47 Thunderbolt pilot in Burma and later a schoolteacher in De Kalb. What a stroke of good luck it was to stumble upon this book! I had heard that there once had been an airport at Waterman, Illinois, just south of De Kalb, but never had any details until that day. The book told the wonderful story of a World War I veteran who raised his family while maintaining an emergency airmail field during the Great Depression of the 1930s. It's a perfect example of the kind of people who conquered the greatest economic disaster of that century and bred what is now called the greatest generation. In addition, an example of the growth of the aviation industry during the Golden Age is told from the Lindbergh era up to World War II. Published in 2001 by the Robbers Roost Press of Edmonds, Washington, it is surely the best description of a family growing up on a little grass airfield this amateur historian has ever read.

ONE PICTURE AND A THOUSAND WORDS

Ted Koston (Costopoulos) was for many years the premiere aerial photographer in the Chicago area. At any aviation event, Ted could be found snapping away and posing groups in front of the most impressive airplane on the field. "One more for the West Coast" was his motto. He was an expert at framing a picture just right. One of the many pictures of his that impressed me was taken at Sky Harbor Airport in Northbrook, Illinois. It shows the flight line there in June 1946 and tells the story of postwar aviation beautifully.

In the foreground is a brand-new sparkling Ercoupe NC99232. This little low-wing tricycle-gear two-seater was looked down on by "real" pilots because it was designed to be flown like a car and quite often was. But it buzzed along at one hundred miles per hour on only four and a half gallons of thirty-cent-a-gallon gasoline and could be put on the ground by even a student pilot in crosswinds that would bedevil most tail-wheel pros. Ironically, fifty years later, it is now a very sought-after aircraft because the earliest models fall into the weight limitations of the Light Sport Aircraft category, which allows pilots who are unable to maintain an airman's medical certificate to fly with merely a driver's license. So, the "hotshot Charleys" of 1946 who looked down their noses at the "scare-coupe" but are now suffering the ravages of time are taking a second look at the "sissy's" airplane.

In the middle of the photo is a line of the perennial Piper J-3 Cub. They have big "buzz" numbers painted on their sides so they could be easily identified if their pilots decided to impress their girlfriends with some low-

Sky Harbor Airport, 1950. *Northbrook Historical Society.*

The Patrushka Club building and a Gray Goose Airlines Ford tri-motor, Sky Harbor, 1930. *B. Thalman.*

altitude shenanigans. Number "5" NC33119 is being hand propped by a line boy in white coveralls. On the back of the coveralls is "Mid-States Avn.," or perhaps "Sky Harbor." Hand propping was considered a common chore for any teenager who haunted the local airport trying to build "time." Eight hours of refueling, stacking and unstacking hangars and washing airplanes could earn fifteen minutes or maybe an hour of flying time. And no "Would you like fries with that?"

George Edgecombe's first flying job, 1933. *George French.*

On the third line of aircraft is a rare plane even for the 1946 period: a Monocoupe NC1002. On its wing tip and fuselage is the insignia of the Civil Air Patrol, a three-bladed propeller inside a white triangle set on a dark blue circle. Powered by a seven-cylinder engine of various horsepower, sometimes with clipped wings, Monocoupes won many air races in the 1930s and, during the war, spotted and sank a few German U-boats off the East Coast. One of the most famous Monocoupe race pilots operated out of the original Aurora Airport (not Sugar Grove) and became the inspiration for a book about a seagull. John Livingston was his name.

And then, far in the background in front of a grove of trees stood a line of war-surplus military-training planes: a North American AT-6 and four Consolidated Vultee BT-13s or maybe navy SNVs. Earl Reinhart and his brother owned a surplus yard across from Pal-Waukee Airport on Palatine Road. Earl was also a partner in the Victory Air Museum near Barrington. In a piece written for the April 1969 Antique Airplane Association newsletter, he speaks of the BTs. Earl wrote:

> *The BT-13 was flown by more cadets of the Air Force and Navy than any other trainer. The first civilian BT to arrive in the Chicago area was flown in by ex-WASP (Women's Air Service Pilot) Jane Page landing at Sky Harbor. In the next five years hundreds of BTs came to the Chicago area to be converted as high powered aircraft. They plagued the airport managers with their noisy buzz jobs but filled their pockets at the gas pumps. The BT was noted for its long range and IFR instrumentation.*
>
> *A noted BT owner was radio announcer Franklin McCormack who in 1946 hit a 2 inch telephone line coming in to Sky Harbor, landed inverted but walked away from it.* [McCormack was heard on the WGN kids after school radio program *Jack Armstrong, the All American Boy*, sponsored by Wheaties, the breakfast of Champions, and later on the WGN *All-Night Showcase*, sponsored by the Peter Hand Brewing Co., makers of Meister Brau beer.] *Johnny Nesbit buzzed the 19th hole at Tam-O-Shanter golf club and brought the farm. Dick Genius, VIP from Fairbanks Morse, ran out of gas on takeoff at O'Hare and landed on the rail road tracks on the west side along York road. BTs were noted mostly for their vibrating high propeller noise and leaking fuel tanks needed re-sealing often. Gas fumes in the cockpit were common. George Hanby of Walgreen Drugs used his BT very efficiently and was the first civilian to make an Instrument approach in this area.*

Sky Harbor Airport, 1946. *Ted Koston.*

    The greatest acrobatics anyone had ever seen since General Udet performed over Curtiss Reynolds airport in the 1930's was performed in a BT-13 by Willis Clark over Pal-Waukee in the late 1940's. Clark had been chief acrobatics instructor at Thunderbird Field in Arizona during WW II and became Chief Instructor for the Associated Flying Clubs of America [to become known later as Sally's Flying Club]. *In the 1950s, a giant fire ball was seen in the sky over Chicago. Marsalis* [sic] *Foose, the "F" in B&F Aircraft at Harlem airport and later 95ᵗʰ street in Oak Lawn, was sky writing in a BT when the engine quit and sucked in a load of paraffin oil used to make smoke and then exploded in a flash! The Nikol brothers were regular commuters in the 1940's. They would take off in a BT from Arlington Heights airport at 2 pm, fly four miles to O'Hare, then return at night. Paul Polidori was known as Mr. BT or as Paul the Painter* [house painter] *and was a man who had made more dead stick landings than he could remember.* [Polidori was another partner in the Victory Air Museum.] *He owned up wards to 20 BTs from 1946 to 1957. Paul's most memorable experience was in a special BT-13 that had been modified to carry a giant folding neon sign attached to the bottom of the plane. It carried such a huge power plant that it could only carry 45 minutes fuel and only a few minutes over its target, down town Chicago at night. On one of these hair raising flights, his engine quite over Niles and he dead sticked it in to Pal-Waukee skidding along the runway in a shower of neon glass. In his own words, a real nightmare!*

BTs became scarce when their 450-horsepower engines also became scarce, and the airplanes were clobbered for their engines. Only two BTs were still flying in the area in the 1960s, according to Earl.

Isn't it amazing what stories can be told by one photograph thanks to the talents of one of the most prolific aerial photographers in the Chicago area, Theodore John Costopoulos (Ted Koston)?

RAVENSWOOD

No other airport in the Chicago area had a more exotic name than the little forty-acre sod field on Touhy Avenue, four miles west of Park Ridge. There doesn't seem to be any connection to the Ravenswood area on Chicago's North Side. Did the trees on the field attract ravens? Certainly, Edgar Allan Poe never heard of it while pondering weak and weary upon a midnight dreary.

While many hundreds of pilots passed through this mysterious airfield, quite a few well-known names in Chicago aviation bounced their wheels there at one time or another. The date of origin of the field is lost in the mists of time, but a September 1930, article in the *Chicago Tribune* reported the crash of a Heath Parasol monoplane powered by a four-cylinder Henderson motorcycle engine. The plane had departed Ravenswood ten minutes earlier, encountered strong winds and spun into a field a mile west of the airport. The article goes on to say that the airport manager, William Turgeon, witnessed the accident. Earlier, Turgeon had been the chief flying instructor at the Chicago Flying Club field at the intersection of Irving Park Road and Thatcher Avenue, and later, in 1938, he would become the guiding hand at Sky Harbor Airport in Northbrook, Illinois. But in the meantime, he taught a fellow named Abe Marmel to fly. Some sources report that Marmel then bought the airport six years later. Even after the close of the field in 1962, Marmel and his wife, Shirley, had the largest stock of Ercoupe airplane parts in the area, if not in the Midwest. Shirley Marmel was listed as the manager

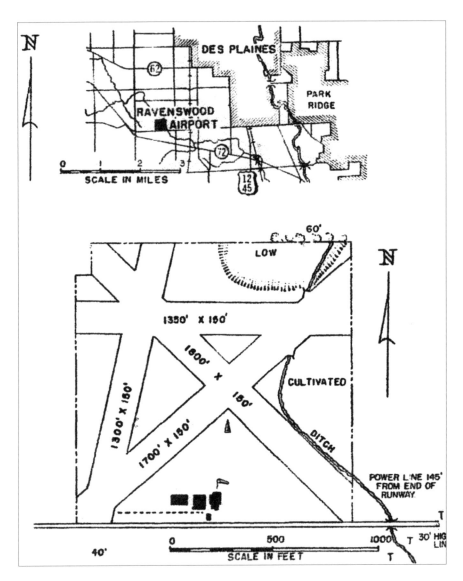

Ravenswood Airport, 1954. *Illinois Airport Directory.*

of the Ravenswood Airport Corporation in a small article in the *Chicago Tribune* dated June 1953, when she was arrested on the charge of possession of gambling devices. Apparently, when business was slow, some airports supplemented their incomes with slot machines and punchboards.

In the early 1940s, George Edgecombe and partner Bob Tufts apparently operated out of Ravenswood. Edgecombe, whose address was given as

Irene Leverton, almost an astronaut, at Elmhurst Airport, 1950s. *Elmhurst Historical Society.*

Des Plaines, Illinois, at the time, won an award in 1940 as one of the top Piper aircraft salesmen and became a member of the "High Hat" club for selling 117 Piper aircraft that year. Edgecombe was another operator who played "musical chairs" as one airport after another succumbed to creeping suburbia, moving to Elmhurst and Elgin in later years.

Although I never flew into Ravenswood, I suspect the pilots trained there were above average because of an unusual terrain feature not found at most airfields. The field started out as an "all-way" airport, as most landing sites were when airplanes had large wheels and could land in almost any meadow. I suppose the trouble and expense of mowing all that grass led to outlining designated landing areas we now call "runways" and cutting the grass only in those areas. This is where the uniqueness of Ravenswood comes in. When laying out the longest northeast-southwest runway, it was necessary to cross a small creek that ran across the field more or less north to south. The solution was a bridge. The runways were 150 feet wide, but there's no info about how wide the bridge was. It probably was no big problem to stay in the middle while crossing the creek, but I wonder how many airplanes ended up "up a creek with no paddle." The east–west runway crossed the diagonal runway at the same point, which probably added a safety factor, too. The longest runway was 1,800 feet, and other obstacles were some electrical wires and a railroad track on the east side. It was said that when taking off east on a hot day, departures were delayed if a train was passing by.

Bob Zilinsky, an A&P mechanic for American Airlines and later a flight engineer, worked part time for Abe Marmel during the 1950s. He related a story about a Navion that landed gear-up and was blocking the runway. Marmel called Zelinski to come out and jack the ship up and off the runway. Bob refused because of high, gusting winds, so Marmel attempted the job himself but ended up with a jack sticking through the wing when the wind did its thing. When the wind died down, Bob came out and unsnarled the job.

Two buddies of mine, who are members of our Friday "lunch bunch" at Clow Airport, shared some memories of flying at Ravenswood just after World War II. John Meyer and Norm Wandke remembered that a portion of the large hanger was used to serve hamburgers and adult beverages after 5:00 p.m. Anne Noggle, a former WASP (Women's Air Force Service Pilot) during the war, later an artist and author, used to partake of boilermakers after a hard day of flight instructing on the field. She signed Norm off on his spot landings in June 1945. To celebrate VJ Day in August, some of the local pilots took off and circled the big radio towers near Route 83 and Thorndale Road. Another noted female pilot, Irene Leverton, took Norm for a ride in a surplus Fairchild PT-19.

Leverton had learned to fly at Elmhurst Airport but soloed at Ravenswood a few years earlier. She tried to enlist in the WASP but was too young. She even tried a forged birth certificate and a "P-51" log book (Parker Pen model 51), but to no avail. At the dedication of Meigs Field in 1948, she flew an Aeronca Ag plane over the crowd and sprayed the assembly with Jacqueline Cochrane's newest perfume, named Pursuit. She went on to a long career in aviation as a charter corporate ferry pilot, U.S. Forest Service pilot, FAA examiner and CAP pilot and almost made it into space in the 1960s when she was selected and trained as one of the Mercury 13 astronauts. It's said that she acquired her desire to fly when her mother took her to an amusement park on Chicago's North Side, probably River View, which had a parachute ride. She also was a defense plant worker briefly at the Douglas plant, helping to build Douglas C-54s as a teenager.

Norm and John recalled a hangar fire at Ravenswood that spread to the C-47 fuselage in which a GI veteran and his wife were living during the postwar housing shortage. To top it off, a local pilot taxied too close to the fire, and embers ignited the fabric on the plane, which burned to a tubular skeleton.

By 1962, the Illinois Airport Directory aerial photograph showed the coming demise of the field. To the north can be seen the newly constructed tollway, while on the west edge of the field one can see the large mobile home park. The traffic pattern had been lowered to four hundred feet to avoid the jets at O'Hare, and two-way radio was required to contact O'Hare before takeoff or landing.

Even after the field had been closed for seventeen years, it burst into newspaper and television news in February 1979, when an American Airlines DC-10 crashed on the remains of the field after takeoff from O'Hare. All aboard the airliner were lost, while Abe Marmel and his wife, who were working in one of the remaining hangar buildings, still building Ercoupes, were spared.

THAT BEAUTIFUL PLACE IN THE COUNTRY

Pal-Waukee

Oh, how can there be any sin in sincere, any good in goodbye or any fair in farewell.
—a barbershop song from another near forgotten era

To a couple kids growing up in the city and the suburbs, driving out to Pal-Waukee was like a breath of fresh air. I had only to drive up the Des Plaines River from Elmwood Park, but Suzette came all the way from the Lake Shore. She was still in high school and had to get a ride from someone, usually her grandparents. Her parents didn't drive. She soloed before she was old enough to get a driver's license. It was a few years before we got together, but I'll always think of Pal-Waukee as more than just trees and grass and open spaces. It was the start of something very special.

In the summer of 1959, I decided I was finally making enough money to begin flying lessons. I had the remainder of my GI Bill left. I had used half of it attending Northrop Aero Institute in California to obtain an A&E ticket from the CAA. I had planned to get on with an airline as a mechanic and begin flying, but the recession of 1957 scuttled that idea. They were only hiring people with fifteen years of experience, so I was working in my brother-in-law's machine shop for minimum wage, seventy-five cents an hour. As appreciative as I was to be working, it was pure drudgery—indoors all day, in the city, facing a brick wall though a dirty window, standing over a lathe machine turning endless boxes of metal parts down to a certain dimension.

Pal-Waukee Airport.

So one fine Sunday afternoon, I appeared at that beautiful country airport on Milwaukee and Palatine Roads. There were three flying schools on the field: George Priester Aviation Service, Sally's Flying Club and Vic Jacobs. I didn't know who was who or where, so I walked into the big white two-story building along Palatine Road and inquired. "Upstairs," I was told. To the left was a barroom (at an airport?) and to the right a restaurant. A center stairway next to a phone booth (remember them?) led up to a flight office with a large picture window overlooking the field. Shortly, I was going out and down an outside circular staircase with my new instructor, Wally Mills. Wally was blond, lanky and perpetually grinning. We walked across the parking lot, past a set of bleacher seats, through a gate in the wire fence and across the ramp to a grassy area where sat several rows of aircraft. The first two rows were yellow J-3 Cubs. The second row all had red bands around the fuselages, just ahead of the fin. Those were Sallys, I later learned. Wally showed me how to pre-flight the ship, sat me in the backseat and propped the N70154 to life. We taxied out, took off and spent an hour in the practice area doing turns, climbs, glides and slow flight. Afterward, I mentioned to Wally that I had an A&E license, and he told me that they were looking for a mechanic in the shop. Joy of joys! Not only was I on my way to a pilot's license, but also I was out of the machine shop. The next day, I started work in the brick hangar next to the beacon tower at twice my wage at the machine shop, $1.90 an hour. The recession was over. Happy days were here again. (That song was from the Depression but certainly fit my mood.)

Probably one of the most unusual features of Pal-Waukee at that time were the parallel runways and traffic pattern. O'Hare had just built its first parallel, 32 left/14 right; Midway had some, too. But I had never seen them before, so it seemed quite novel to me at the time. Pal-Waukee had two sets of parallels: 06/24 left and right and 12/30 left and right. All were paved but the Cub runways; 6 right/24 left and 30 left /12 right were narrower and cinder on tar rather than asphalt. The school trainers and anything under one hundred horsepower used the Cub runways. Bigger ships and transients used the big runways but often taxied back on the Cub runways, mistaking them for a parallel taxiway in spite of the fact that there might be half a dozen Cubs in the Cub pattern. Keep in mind, this was long before the control tower was built. The only communication link was that newfangled thing called "Unicom" on 122.8 mega cycles.

I don't think any other airport offered the variety of aircraft as did Priester Aviation Service. The standard trainer, of course, was the Piper J-3 Cub, of which half a dozen were available. Two Piper PA-18 Super Cubs with 108-horsepower Lycoming engines gave a fellow a little edge on cross-country trips with a head wind. These were unusual in that they had toe brakes instead of the heel pedals of the J-3s. And they rented for the same price, eight bucks an hour, wet and solo. In addition, there were two PA-12 Super Cruisers (I thought this was the Cadillac of the Piper line when I checked out in it), two Cessna 140s, two straight-tail Cessna 172s, a C-182 and two "C" model Bonanzas with the electric props. The Cessnas (except for the 140s) and the Bonanzas all had radios. The two Super Cruisers had Hallicrafter low-frequency radios in the middle of the instrument panel, but the local-range stations had been decommissioned recently, so they merely filled the hole in the panel. The elite of the fleet were twin-engine jobs and a Stearman, a Beech 18, a Cessna 310, a Piper Apache and a Grumman Widgeon. Oh, yes. There was an Ercoupe as well. The radios of the era were very unique. The Lear LTVR, for instance, had two tunable receivers, one for low frequency and one for VHF. The transmitter had maybe six different Crystals. Narco had many different models—the Omnigator, the Superhomer and the Omniplexer—and they all weighed ten or twelve pounds.

The C-310 in particular was a very slick-looking machine. It had a paint scheme that was quite outstanding, a sort of 1950s art deco—dark red with white and black trim. It had a straight tail, over-wing "echo can" augmenter exhaust tubes and uncanted tip tanks. George Priester had an incident in the 310 that was impressive to all who witnessed it. While aloft one day in the early 1960s, the landing gear failed and could not be hand cranked. On final approach to runway 30R, he shut off both engines, bumped the starters until the props were horizontal and set it down on the grass next to the runway with hardly a scratch. He was already respected as the "Boss," the airport owner and a pilot examiner, but after that exhibit of airmanship, I thought he was Lindbergh, Doolittle and "Smilin' Jack" all in one!

Probably the largest airplane on the field was the Consolidated PBY Catalina, a model -5A, I believe, with retractable landing gear. It was painted yellow with white trim, and sitting near a line of yellow J-3s, it looked like mama duck and her ducklings. As I recall, it was to be used as an aerial broadcasting station for the new PBS TV station. This was probably before the big antennas were built on the John Hancock or Sears building in downtown Chicago. The PBY could stay airborne for twenty-two hours, I was told, and had bed bunks and an electric galley.

Surely the most unusual aircraft in the Priester stable was a German-powered soaring plane called the Rhine Flugzubaur RW-3. This was a steel tube fuselage covered with formed fiberglass panels, with two tandem seats under a sliding bubble canopy, powered by a seventy-five-horsepower Porsche air-cooled four-cylinder engine behind the rear seat. A drive shaft extended back to the pusher propeller mounted between the vertical fin and the rudder. It sat on tricycle retractable landing gear. The normal wingspan was about forty feet, but extensions could be installed to make it about seventy-two feet. When it first came on the line, Jack Layer and I gave it a try. Jack had instructed in Stearmans during the war; he had a gray crew cut, a perpetual grin and was an all-around good guy. And very soft-spoken. We took it up to about four thousand feet and did a few spins, left and right. I don't think we shut off the engine and tried soaring (I would have remembered that!). It was a hazy day with no raising air. I do remember that the empty weight was the same as a Stearman, about 1,900 pounds, so I expect it was more of a glider rather than a soaring plane.

For a short time, one of the strangest airplanes we ever saw was at Pal-Waukee, a twin-engine Aeronca Champion called a "Lancer." It had a one-hundred-horsepower Continental engine hung on each wing with fixed-pitch wood props, fixed landing gear and a control wheel in the front seat with a stick in the back. You could actually get a multi-engine rating in it.

I was privileged to work with some very sharp and experienced mechanics in the brick hangar. Milt Garner was a quiet and religious man, quite a gardener, tall and lean. Johnnie Rompa was a well-fed comical fellow who had been a mechanic on Stearmans during the war. He had two young daughters at the time, and they lived at "forty square," by Chicago street numbers, Irving Park Road and Pulaski Avenue. His favorite expression was: "There's only one solution and that's a liquid." Go figure. Eddy "Cornflakes" Conifise was as quiet as Milt and very skillful. He did all the fabric work on the Cubs and built terrific model airplanes. His sister, Martha, worked the desk in the flight office and the Unicom radio. She was outgoing and gregarious. (Being a dance band buff, whenever I hear that Larry Clinton tune sung by Bea Wayne, "Oh, Martha," I'm reminded of her.) Martha's husband, Harry Gunther, was the parts manager in the shop. Whatever part you needed, he had the number for it and knew where to get it. Sometimes all he had to do was go across Palatine Road to the Reinhart brothers' salvage yard. They had a Grumman Wildcat, I think it was, parked in front. Next to them was the Rupert Parachute and Seat Belt Co. Harry and Martha flew a neat little blue-and-white Piper Clipper and drove a little MG, I believe, on road rallies. Bill Stevens was another sharp guy, a naval reservist at Glenview and, later, the flight engineer on the Chicago White Sox's DC-7. He and his wife and two sons lived in the farmhouse along Milwaukee Road near the end of runway 06L.

It was really a family airport at that time. Mr. Priester was the owner and pilot examiner. Mrs. Priester and her two daughters, Sheila and Sharon, often worked the schedule desk, and son Charlie flew charters and instructed. A photo by Ted Koston shows a small wooden building in the parking lot where, I'm told, "the kids" used to sell ice cream. It was later replaced with a set of bleacher seats. Charlie was, and probably still is, an energetic guy, full of pep. He had a bounce to his step, always on his toes. I imagine the marines had a hard time getting him to march in a military way. One of the girls, I forgot which, used to trade "Swiftys" with me. Tom Swift was a boy inventor in a series of books from an earlier age that was unique in its written prose. The object was to match the quotation with an adverb. She always topped me.

Another naval reservist named John, whose last name I have forgotten, worked part time, and he and I were changing a couple cylinders on the left engine of the PBY when he related some interesting stories. First, a little background.

The PBY Catalina had two radial engines, P&W 1830s, I believe, mounted on the wing, which was atop a pylon amidships on the fuselage. They were maybe fifteen or eighteen feet above the ground, but up there it looked like fifty feet. (Have you ever noticed that many flyers have a fear of heights when not at the controls?) The engine nacelles had little panels that folded out and became work platforms and allowed maintenance to be done without tall work stands or ladders.

During the course of our cylinder change, several nuts, bolts and wrenches were dropped (mostly by me; John was more experienced), requiring a rather circuitous route to retrieve same. It was up onto the nacelle, over the wing to the pylon, down the pylon to the hull (fuselage), down the hull to the landing gear tire, hop to the ground, find and pick up the item and back up again. A hop, skip and a jump for a guy in his twenties but a pain in the neck for a short-tempered young "kraut head." After several such trips, John, an older and wiser veteran of the South Pacific, said to me, "How would you like to be working on one of these ships at anchor in some lagoon, bobbing up and down with each wave, and every time you dropped something, it was the deep six!" While I was picturing this, John further explained that to avoid such situations, they would sling a tarp under the engine, but often it would fill with oil. This made retrieving tools a shorter trip but became a chore called "pearl diving." The job was completed with a lot less moaning on my part.

John also told me of a whole squadron of PBYs at anchor in a lagoon when a typhoon came up. The wind was so strong that the lines attached to the bow of the planes pushed the nose hatches under water, and the whole fleet sank. After the repairs had been made, several of us were invited to take a ride. (It wasn't until many years later that I learned why mechanics were often invited on test flights.) I jumped at the chance, of course. It was the loudest and noisiest airplane I've ever been on. All those flight crews of World War II must be deaf as doornails. Mr. Priester let me sit in the left seat for ten minutes. I tried a left turn. Many seconds later, the wing responded. The men who flew those things must have had biceps like grapefruits. I heard later that they tried landing on Lake Michigan—once! It started taking on water, so they lifted right off. Who knows?

Once we had our commercial licenses, it was customary to hang around the flight office to build up flying time by taking passenger hops. One cold but sunny Sunday afternoon, a young couple bought a twenty-minute ride, and I was next up. You have undoubtedly heard that old saw: "There are those who have and those who will land gear-up." Well, I came close! The only ship available was one of the "C" model Bonanzas (maybe 10 Alpha, the brown one). Only it had a dead battery. No problem. Tony Nichol or maybe his brother, Otto, the twenty-four-seven line department at Priesters, easily hand propped it, and off we went to circle the Bahia Temple on the lakeshore and back. With the electric prop, the Lear radio and the electric landing gear motor, something had to give—and it did. The gear stopped halfway up, and I heard Wally Mills on the Unicom almost in a whisper, "Your gear is not all the way up." No problem, right? I'm a mechanic. I don't need no stinkin' motor! (That movie actually came out several years later.) So I reached over the seat back near my passengers' feet and cranked up the gear by hand. (You're not supposed to do that.) Coming back, I cranked the gear down (its OK to do it that way) and lined up for runway 30R. Over Palatine Road, I heard this funny whirling noise. My mechanical training immediately clicked into action: the gear was coming up! My pilot training kicked into action: I went around. Circling the field, it dawned on me. I had left the gear selector in the "UP" position, and the circuit breaker, which was of the automatic thermal reset type, had reset itself after it cooled, right over Palatine Road. It was a classic case of being so smart, I outsmarted myself. To this day, I bet the young couple in back wondered why their pilot was trying to play footsie with them.

THE CIVIL AIR PATROL
TO THE RESCUE

B ack in the last century (sounds ancient, doesn't it?), Suzette and I belonged to the Suburban Aviation Flying Club, which had been around the Chicago area since the 1950s. On one particular occasion, our monthly fly-out was to Madison, Wisconsin. An arts and craft show was held on the streets around the State Capitol Building. A nice afternoon was had by all, until we returned to Truex Field. A check of the Teletype machine (remember them?) revealed that the weather back in Chicago had not lived up to the forecast. (Imagine that.) All stations back home were reporting overcast skies at six hundred feet and three miles visibility in light rain. Our bright, sunny morning had suckered me into leaving our approach plates and charts behind. I borrowed some plates from the local FBO and Xeroxed (another machine from the past) the approach to Du Page Airport. Its localizer approach would get us down below the reported ceiling. The VOR approach to our home field was too high.

The other planes had already filed their flight plans, so by the time we filed ours, we were assigned five thousand feet. Sue and I had topped the tanks after arrival, so with two backseat passengers, we were about at gross weight. And it began drizzling as we loaded up.

With the moderate temperature and high humidity, our climb rate left something to be desired. This was also before the requirement for an encoding transponder. The controller must have asked us a dozen times if we were at five thousand yet. We finally leveled off and built up cruise speed, a whopping 105 miles per hour! We crept pass Janesville and Rockford.

CAP member Fernwegner at Sky Haven Airport, 1940s. *Karen Fernwegner.*

Flying toward a low-pressure area, we had a left quartering head wind and wet, soggy clouds.

Our 1948 Stinson Station Wagon at that time was equipped with a Narco Mk. 12, 360 channel Nav./Comm. with a localizer but no glide slope. It also had a Terra transistorized Nav./Comm. (very up to date) and a Marker beacon receiver. The transponder had a power supply under the pilot's seat, and the Narco had another power supply on the firewall above the rudder pedals. You can see why our use full load was limited. Fortunately, when I had re-covered the ship with new fabric several years earlier, I had scraped several layers of enamel paint off the sheet metal and had removed about twenty pounds from the airplane's empty weight.

Although I had been an instrument flight instructor for some ten years, I rarely flew with backseat passengers to contend with. However, our two backseaters were both pilots. Bob Beyer was a longtime flyer, and Bev Meyer had soloed a J-3 Cub. Due to the lack of scenery throughout the trip, they dozed most of the way. My co-captain, Suzette, had learned to fly as a teenager and was instrument rated but would much rather watch the passing parade on the ground. So she kept track of our position on the chart while looking for a break in the clouds. But none appeared.

Finally, we intercepted the localizer for runway ten at Du Page and were cleared for the approach. We broke out of the clouds into a light rain just past the outer marker with the Fox River in sight. The controller in the tower knew me and our bright yellow Stinson. I commuted daily via airplane to my job on the field, but rarely in such weather.

After splashing down on the runway, we taxied to the north ramp. Barely had the prop stopped revolving when we all echoed the same thought: "How do we get home?" Our cars were twelve miles away. Almost immediately, a van drove up in the parking lot behind us, and out stepped our neighbor, Ron Westholm. Ron and his wife, Florence, lived up the street on Aero Drive at Naper Aero Estates. They were both longtime members of the Dowers Grove Squadron of the Civil Air Patrol. Ron had been working on one of the CAP ships in a hangar facing the runway we had just alighted upon and was curious about how our normally fair-weather Stinson had gotten into such a sloppy fix. And by the way, "Would you like a ride home?"

This little story is not meant to belittle the tremendous job the CAP does. Since before World War II, the volunteers of the CAP have saved many, many lives and performed all sorts of services during floods, storms and other disasters and emergencies with little or no recognition. And they continue to do so in this digital twenty-first century.

THE COUNTRY CLUB AIRPORTS

It's not generally known, but the three pioneer airports of the North Shore area of Chicago were planned as palatial getaways for the affluent population of Lake Forest, Glencoe, Glenview and other beautiful northern suburbs. Pal-Waukee, Curtiss Reynolds and Sky Harbor were all products of the Jazz Age and the bull stock market.

Pal-Waukee was opened in 1925 by Roy E. Guthier, a pilot of the Great War. It carried that name for some time before taking the name of the two intersecting roads on which it bordered: Milwaukee and Palatine. In 1919, Guthier gave instruction to Ed Heath, father of the home-built kit plane. In 1928, Owen Barton Jones and two other Lake Forest men purchased Pal-Waukee and began putting money into it. This evidently showed some dividends, as some prominent sportsmen-pilots began basing their airplanes there. Unfortunately, a fire erupted on Christmas Eve 1930, and seventeen planes were destroyed. Among the plane owners were Colonel Robert R. McCormick, publisher of the *Chicago Tribune*; Fred Foote, business manager of *Life* magazine; and Forest Mars, president of Mars Candy Co. Chester Foust, a lesser-known advertising agent perhaps but a very interesting writer, lost an Avro Avian and a Waco in the blaze.

It was a couple articles in the *Sportsman Pilot* magazine by Foust in the mid-1930s that brought the Chicago Aviation Country Club (ACC) into the light of the present day for this amateur historian. The editors of the *Sportsman Pilot* credited Foust as being the moving spirit of the ACC. His home was

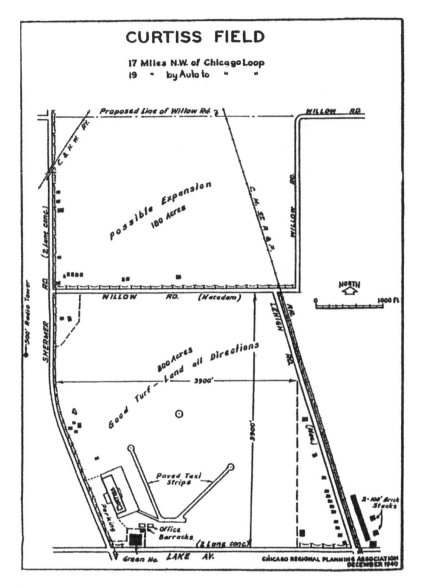

Curtiss Field, 1940.

on an estate he called a farm outside Lake Forest, and he used his airplane extensively in his business travels around the country. He raised Bedlington terriers and was a deputy sheriff in Lake County. He was in the navy in the war (the First World War) and became a Great Lakes yachtsman, so he didn't learn to fly until 1929. His fellow sportsmen-pilots say that without

Sky Harbor Airport, 1941. *Finzer.*

him, the ACC would never have come into being. It was he who talked Owen Jones into a lease for the ACC.

One particular item credited to him struck a note with this knuckle-buster and (thank God) ex-smoker. Foust is the fellow who sold the Camel Cigarette Company on the idea of wrapping its packages of coffin nails in cellophane. It was common practice in that era to time a magneto or a distributor by inserting a bit of cellophane between the breaker points. A steady pull on the cellophane, which was only about a half-thousandth of an inch thick, as you rotated the mag would tell you when the points were about to open. This was probably the only worthwhile use for a pack of cigarettes.

In the October 1934 issue of the *Sportsman Pilot*, Foust tells, in a very amusing manner, of the origin of the ACC. One of the future members, Lloyd Laflin, tried to satisfy both of his favorite hobbies one cloudless Sunday morning. He wanted to fly his new Waco model D biplane and also attend the opening foxhunt at Milburn, Illinois. Dressed in his hunt club habit of red coat, breeches and boots, he drove like mad to Pal-Waukee from Lake Forest, mounted the Waco and flew off. The airport manager and veteran transport pilot, Cliff Condit, spent the rest of the day and a whole bottle of post-Prohibition hooch placating the Lake Forest Police and Lake County sheriff, who had arrived as Laflin ascended. Upon Laflin's return later that afternoon, a remark made by one of the departing deputies—something about "this must be some kind of a country club"—sparked the idea, and two days later, the Chicago Aviation Country Club was incorporated.

Twenty members were invited to join at $120 annually, and Department of Commerce mechanics were made available. Two more department mechanics who turned to home cooking when the "slump" (read, "crash") in the stock market occurred leased the second floor of the administration building. The second floor also had clubrooms, locker and washrooms, a lounge and an office. The first-floor restaurant and bar were open to the public, while a dumbwaiter served the club room lounge.

Foust describes Laflin's red Waco as the flagship of the ACC. In his droll sense of humor, he describes it as able to penetrate fog by its ruby radiance alone. Another member, Wayne King, the bandleader known as "the Waltz King," flew a "steam-heated" Stinson Reliant but was looking to trade for a fast, open job. Some sportsmen-pilots believed cabin jobs were "sissy ships," said Faust. "And why didn't YOU keep up your music lessons?" Instruction was offered in Manager Condit's Fleet biplane. Harry Georgeiff, chief mechanic at the Sikorsky ramp at the World's Fair on the Chicago lakefront (the Century of Progress Fair celebrating Chicago's 100th birthday) became the club's first student and soloed in ten days.

(A Pal-Waukee Airport Corporation concession operated two Sikorsky S-38 twin-engine amphibians on sightseeing trips between the fair and Curtiss Reynolds Airport.)

The purpose of the ACC was not entirely social. Even the affluent members of the North Shore were feeling the effects of the stock market crash of 1929, and by combining resources and cutting costs, the members were able to fly and operate their aircraft economically and still enjoy an aeronautical fraternity.

An advertisement in the December 1935 issue of the *Sportsman Pilot* told of Chicago's Aviation Country Club, located at Pal-Waukee Airport, northwest of the city at number two airway beacon, Chicago–Milwaukee route, on the west bank of the Des Plaines River. Look for the blimp hangar—full service for the private owner; convenient to all North Shore towns; station wagon to railroad or city. The first night of storage was free to all SPA and PFA; it was outside the smoke zone and offered full weather information.

The SPA (Sportsman Pilot Association) and PFA (Private Pilot Association) were popular flying clubs of the 1930s. The blimp hangar referred to was a two-blimp shed erected by the Goodyear Company and used to transport visitors to the Century of Progress World's Fair held in 1932 and 1933. It was still standing in a photograph taken in 1937. It was likely torn down during one of the many scrap drives in World War II.

The lack of greater success of the ACC was attributed, by some, to the close location of three other fields. These were Sky Harbor, Curtiss Reynolds and Park Ridge. A notation in the September 1936 issue of *Popular*

Aviation magazine explained that the Chicago Aviation Country Club was originally intended to duplicate the fashionable and successful Long Island Aviation Country Club at Hicksville, New York. However, few activities such as the aerial vacation flights of the Long Island club or their mass flight visits to members' homes or estates had been undertaken by the Chicago group.

Sky Harbor began its own Aviation Country Club in 1941 by introducing and dedicating a new hangar. It is believed to be the hangar just north of the 1930 hangar in the northeast corner of the field along Antony Road. However, the clubrooms were located on the east side of the original hangar. This might have been where the Ceiling Zero restaurant was in later years. A souvenir program describes the club's purpose:

> *This is to be the focal point for North Shore aviation enthusiasts. It is here where much of the day's hangar flying will be done and where wives can wait for their husbands to return from business trips on which they fly at the controls of their own ships. It also will serve as a friendly hospitable spot in which to relax and chat with friends while waiting for good weather or just as a place where one can find congenial people whose interest is in aviation. Membership in the Aviation Country Club is restricted to men only; however, the ladies are by no means neglected. Most of the cruises, breakfast flights, etc. are co-educational and on alternate Sundays, various members donate their services and provide an afternoon of bridge and entertainment for wives and guests.*

The program went on to say:

> *It is appropriate that Aviation Country Club, whose very purpose is to co-ordinate social activity in to the busy life of today's airport, should with this hangar warming party dedicate this fine new hangar into the service of today's aviation activities. May it serve us and our equipment well.*

William R. Turgeon was listed as one of the ten directors, and J.M. Klapp was president of the club. Also listed were Hugh Riddle and Burt Dickens, who were to be founders of Midway Airlines after the war. The coming of war to the United States in December 1941 most likely accounted for the short life of the club, as well as the dated and restricted lifestyle. Bill Trugeon, who came to Sky Harbor in 1937 with a group of investors, managed the airport until its closing in the 1970s. As did most other airports in the Chicago area, Sky Harbor trained pilots for the navy during World

War II. An advertisement from a major magazine of the era found at the Northbrook Historical Society shows Dorothy Ring, U.S. civilian flying instructress, at Sky Harbor in 1941. Dorothy states that she started each day with a bowl of Kellogg's Corn Flakes with fruit and lots of milk.

Curtiss Reynolds Airport, which became Glenview Naval Air Station years later, was only one of a grand plan of the Curtiss Wright Corporation to cover the country with airports and flying schools in the late 1920s. Following Lindbergh's solo Atlantic flight, the Curtiss Company planned to build a nationwide chain of modern airports and service facilities that would be the aviation centers of the future. This chain was to include fifteen cities, one of which was the North Shore area of Chicago, near Glenview. At one time, negotiations were entered into with the possibility of placing an airfield adjacent to the Arlington Park Racetrack.

A publication of the Curtiss Wright Company entitled *Tradewind*, dated May 1930, depicted a giant Curtiss Condor transport biplane on its cover and a list of Wright Aeronautical Corporation–approved service stations on the back cover. The inside described the exciting new world of aviation to the public. A centerfold showed pictures of various modern airport accommodations across the country with their comfortable lounges, waiting rooms and dining solons. The observation tower and protected passenger-boarding ramp with promenade enclosure of the Grand Central Air Terminal at Glendale, Los Angeles, California, was front and center in the collage. Old film buffs will recognize it from many Hollywood flying movies, especially the classic *Casablanca*. The Promenade Deck overlooking the Curtiss Airport at Glenview was also featured. It went on to say:

> *The modern airport is an interesting place where we can see the planes come in. The airport is stepping in where the small town railroad depot left off and is going on from there in a most efficient and satisfying way with an eye to comfort and beauty. Balconies overlooking the landing fields, summer gardens, attractive waiting rooms with windows facing the runways, gaily striped umbrellas to sit under while we sip ice cold lemonade* [Prohibition, you know]; *these and many other features have been provided to while away the time between planes.*

"See Chicago from the Air," spouted an advertisement by the Curtiss Wright Flying Company during the Great Depression. Local sightseeing tours were available for five dollars, and special night aerial tours over Chicago and the suburbs could be had for ten dollars. All flights started from the magnificent new Curtiss Airport at Glenview. "Take the train from Union depot to Glenview station. By motor, take Waukegan Road, turn west at Glenview," the ad went on. So although no formal "country club" was ever formed at Curtiss-Reynolds, it offered the amenities of one to those who could afford them during the poor economy of the 1930s.

Until the coming of World War II, the outstanding event occurring at Curtiss-Reynolds was the National Air Races held there in 1930 and 1933. The Travel Air "Mystery Plane," sponsored by the Texaco Company, was so named because it was hidden away in a hangar until race time. It can still be seen at the Museum of Science and Industry in Chicago. However, the winner of the first Thompson Trophy race in 1930 was a biplane built by Matty Laird at Ashburn field on Chicago's South Side. It was named "The Solution" in reference to the Mystery Plane. Similar to some movie scripts of the era, it was built in a month, some say, and arrived at the races after a ten-minute test flight on the way from Ashburn; its race number was painted on it while lining up for the race start.

Of course, Curtiss-Reynolds became the center of Naval Aviation Training during World War II, but the army operated there before the navy moved in. Stan Tonkin, one of our longtime neighbors at Naper Aero Estates, started as an apprentice mechanic at Curtiss in 1938. His boss, Harold Darr, managed both Pal-Waukee and Curtiss Reynolds at the time, and Stan worked at both airports. In 1939, Darr got a contract to teach army cadets. They had a fleet of Stearman PT-13s; an army barracks was built, and instructors and mechanics were hired. Stan earned his A&E license and the military equivalent, which he later put to good use servicing B-24 bombers. One of the many slide pictures Stan took over the years showed a Stearman up on its nose on a grass field with nothing but trees in the background. On the yellow wings can be seen "ASK" and "N9652H." Stan made his first parachute jump at Curtiss and his second on his eightieth birthday in Florida when he became a "UFO" (unidentified flying octogenarian).

There are many more stories stemming from these three airfields, and I hope to track down some more for future chapters of *Forgotten Chicago Airfields*.

THE VALENTINE BOMBER

Sky Harbor Airport

One of the many stories bandied about the coffee shop/saloon at Pal-Waukee Airport in the early 1960s concerned a navy bomber that landed by mistake there instead of at nearby Glenview Naval Air Station. Sometimes the airport mentioned was Pal-Waukee, sometimes Chicagoland Airport, but in reality it was Sky Harbor.

The Northbrook Historical Society yielded a rather sarcastic short article from a local newspaper that shed some light on the story. The bomber had landed at Sky Harbor, not Pal-Waukee, and was flown back to Glenview the next day. Many years later, I learned more details from a group called the Glenview Survivors, mostly ex-navy men who had served at one time or other at Glenview. These veterans met for lunch and bull shooting at the Old Country Buffet on Golf Road once a month and perhaps still do. But sadly, their ranks are growing thinner and their memories dimmer.

The bomber was a PB4Y Privateer, which was the navy version of the army four-engine B-24. The main visible difference was a single vertical stabilizer instead of the twin fin on the army plane. It had a 110-foot wingspan and weighed sixty thousand pounds normally but fortunately was only forty-five thousand pounds, as it was sinking into the soft runway at Sky Harbor on the night of February 14, 1954, Valentine's Day.

One of the Glenview Survivors I met told me he had been the flight engineer on that bomber and that they had left Jacksonville, Florida, on that day for Glenview. The engineer was carrying an engagement ring he had purchased in Florida and planned to deliver it to his girl on Valentine's night.

The weather was clear as they arrived over Chicago that night, but the number three engine was feathered, and the landing gear had to be pumped down, he told me (but didn't explain why). The copilot was flying and made the first approach, but the captain ordered a go-around. The captain made the second approach and a full-stop landing. They were in radio contact with Glenview tower, and when told to flash their lights so the tower could see them, suspicions began to arise. The tower could not see them. Remember now, at that time, before the Interstate highways and all, it was pretty dark along Dundee Road and was very much boondocks. As the wheels sank slowly into the soft Sky Harbor runway, the engineer called a cab and delivered the ring just before midnight. Did they live happily ever after? Who knows? Was this guy pulling my leg? Probably. But I'll listen to anybody.

Many more years later, one of my good buddies on the graveyard shift at ORD told me he was one of the naval reservists who were ordered to Sky Harbor on the morning after the surprise arrival. They unloaded everything they could to lighten the ship and towed it out of the holes the wheels had made in the runway, then flew it home.

WASHINGTON PARK AIRPORT

Homewood, Illinois

This "ghost airport" is a typical example of the part these little grass fields played in preparing our country for the world conflict developing in the late 1930s. In the summer of 1939, seven local pilots flying from the Chicago Heights Airport decided it was too crowded for what they had in mind and began searching for a new flying site. The Chicago Heights field was situated around a golf course with little room for expansion. Whether these men were merely forming a flying club or had grander ideas concerning the government's new Civilian Pilot Training Program is left to speculation.

In the meantime, during the summer and fall of 1939, Arthur Schweer, Leo Zizic of Crete, George Hanson of Chicago Heights and four others leased 160 acres of hayfields southeast of Homewood from the Leising Lumber Company of Chicago Heights and began preparing it for use as an airfield. This was a half-mile-square parcel on Halsted Street at 187th, extending west to what became Center Street. Apparently, it took several months to fill in holes and level off high spots so that planes would not stub their toes and flip over. Although many airfields at that time were what were called "all-way fields," meaning airplanes could land and take off in whatever direction the wind blew, the men cut the grass along several runways. They were 125 feet wide and outlined with limestone for daylight operations. Kerosene smudge pots were used for night flying. Also, it was quite common to exchange wheels for skis in winter. Many pilots of that era soloed on ski planes. This is an oddity. A special rating is required for seaplane pilots but not for ski planes.

Washington Park Airport, Homewood, Illinois, 1940s. *Jim Wright.*

(Shh! Don't give them any ideas!) Herman Engels of Crete built two wooden hangars. One of them had an office and repair shop, as well as a small control tower. It was not until December 1939 that the State of Illinois and the Civil Aeronautics Administration gave their permission to open the field.

Probably hoping to capitalize on the popularity of the racetrack a mile and a half north, the field was named Washington Park instead of Homewood. And it's entirely possible that the racetrack was an investor in the airport's lease. Who knows? A shuttle service was established between the field and the racetrack as well.

The Washington Park Race Track opened in 1926 and survived for fifty years. Nearby was a dog-racing track and around that a larger auto and motorcycle track. So there was plenty of action in the area.

The August 1, 1941 edition of the *Homewood-Flossmoor Star* carried an article stating that visitors were already crowding the town in anticipation of the coming race season. Merchants reported an increase in business over the 1940 season, and many residents were renting rooms to guests. In another article, it was announced that a new hangar was being built at the Washington Park Airport and forty additional acres of land added to the field. The management was expecting a heavy increase in business due to the arrival of many ships owned by persons attending the horse races. Planes from many states and cities used the airport in 1940, and more were expected in 1941. At the end of this article was a notation that Liewelyn Williams of Chicago and three other students of the present government training class had soloed within the past two weeks.

A surprising little-known fact was revealed in a third article in the same edition. It stated that the Flossmore Boy Scouts were rounding up scrap aluminum for use in the national defense campaign. What is surprising is that

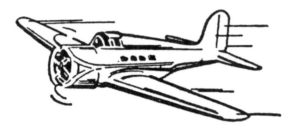
Washington Park Airport advertisement, 1940s. *Jim Wright.*

this was before the Pearl Harbor attack. Another precaution taken, I found, was that airport locations were deleted from all road maps during the war.

The *Chicago Heights Town Crier* (published every Thursday morning, three cents per copy, ten cents per month), on September 24, 1942, announced in big, bold headlines: "ARMY PILOT SCHOOL HERE." Ground school was to be held at Glenwood Manual Training Schools, while flight training would be at the Washington Park Airport. Training was to begin the following Monday and would be very intensive, meaning that when one eight-week course ended, the next would follow immediately. The course would consist of thirty hours of ground school and five to six hours of flight time each week, as well as military drill. This was to replace the Civilian Pilot Training Program previously conducted by Thornton Junior College and other agencies. The students were to be those applicants for flight training who did not meet the rigid requirements for combat pilots. These pilots would be called "service pilots" and would be assigned to the ferry and transport command. Glider pilots would also be trained. At this time, as mentioned elsewhere, the flight instructors at the airport, as well as those all over the country, had to be reinstated. This meant a period of retraining, no matter how long an instructor had been flying and teaching, to ensure that everyone was teaching the same curriculum.

Although service pilots were considered noncombat, this meant only that they could not shoot back at those who were shooting at them. Although the ferry pilots might have been considered the safest branch of the three, they quite often were assigned to target-towing duties for artillery and aerial gunnery schools. More than one of these noncombatants was shot out of the skies by friendly fire. The transport pilots had to contend with atrocious weather over uncharted routes such as the North Atlantic or the Burma Road. And the glider pilots—but I digress.

After the war, the field settled into a civilian routine, with flight training under the GI Bill and a few air shows. The survey conducted to find a replacement for Midway Airport in 1946 stated that Washington Park was twenty-five miles from the Loop and could be reached in fifty minutes by automobile, forty minutes by rail and fifty minutes by bus. Aeronautical activities included charter, training, transient and executive, with thirty planes based on the field. Services included major and minor engine and aircraft repair, storage and fueling. Plans for expansion might be hampered by traffic at nearby Ashland and Rubinkam, it was noted.

But fate had other plans for Washington Park Airport, it would seem. On August 5, 1947, during a nocturnal storm, a lightning bolt struck one of the hangars and demolished it and the eighteen planes inside it. Jess Whitmore, the night watchman, was alerted at about 4:30 a.m., when the airport watchdog, a Kerry blue terrier, started barking. Whitmore called the fire department, and he and the dog made their way to safety through the smoke and flames. For some reason, the terrier ran back into the hangar and perished. Another bolt struck the Glenwood Manual Training School across Halsted Street. The fuel tanks of the planes in the hangar began exploding, and although the Homewood Fire Department arrived within fifteen minutes, it was useless to even hook up the hoses. The firemen were able to save one plane, a Vultee, which was tied down outside the hangar. Eleven Taylorcrafts, two Stearmans and a Piper Cub owned by the airport were lost, as were four privately owned ships. These were a Culver Cadet owned by Dr. H.A. Stevenson, a Harvey dentist; a Stinson owned by Michael Newbury of Chicago; a Fairchild owned by Harold Hawley; and an Ercoupe belonging to E.M. Ward of Chicago. About a dozen ships tied down along the highway were not harmed.

Also destroyed were all the company records and the pilots' log books. However, Miss Doris Hansen, an airport employee, was said to be able to partially recompile the records and logs. Arthur Schweer of Crete, president of Washington Park Airport, Inc., and George Hansen Jr., vice-president, were said to be contemplating rebuilding and restoring service. Meanwhile, the nearby Scheck Engine Shop would house the airport office and contain the GI Flight Program.

Faced with two blazes at the same time, the Homewood Fire Department called for help from Chicago Heights, Homewood Acres, Sunnycrest, Holbrook and Harvey, said Chief N.W. Kuhn. (Information about the fire was taken from the *Chicago Heights Star* of Tuesday, August 5, 1947.)

One could hope that all lived happily ever after—but they did so only for a short while, I'm afraid.

On Tuesday, February 7, 1950, the fickle finger of fate struck again at Washington Park. About 1:30 p.m., David Vallo of Markham, an experienced mechanic and pilot, discovered the flames that soon engulfed the entire hangar and office building. Possibly a spark or a welding torch had ignited the fabric of one of the planes. The fire spread quickly up the wood walls and to the ceiling. Soon, the gas tanks began exploding, and the thick black smoke could be seen for miles. Once again, Miss Doris Hansen, secretary and flight school registrar, made several trips into the burning building to save log books and records, but many were lost. One plane was saved, but many more were lost.

For two years after the war, aircraft manufacturers turned out planes by the thousands for the returning servicemen. A helicopter was predicted for every garage. But not all the ex-aviators could afford an airplane, an education and a family at the same time. In 1947, airplane ramps were saturated with unsold planes, which was a shame because dozens of new designs were developed. Only a few made it into production. It was another ten or fifteen years before general aviation again began to boom. By that time, Washington Park Airport was a thing of the past. Even the racetrack is gone, burned to the ground in 1977.

However, two people survived all this tragedy and lived to see the twenty-first century—Arthur Schweer's wife, Emma, and Leo Zizic's wife, Mary Ann. Both were licensed pilots and members of the 99s, the noted female flyers' organization. Art and Emma operated an appliance store in Crete, and when the airport opened, Emma took over the store. She was also active in the Civil Air Patrol. She had learned to fly in the 1930s, and she and her husband flew together as often as the running of the airport allowed. Art was the township tax collector, and upon his death in the 1960s, Emma was appointed by the township to the job. Township old-timers remember that Emma was "a friendly lady, who never had a hair out of place, was impeccably dressed, wore three-inch high heel shoes and drove a Cadillac."

So, for a short time, Washington Park Airport, along with many others like it, contributed to the winning of World War II.

James Wright of Homewood, author of the book *Homewood Through the Years*, supplied the information that made this story possible. And he's not even a pilot but a very good historian.

Another pilot rating issued to army aviators during World War II was "liaison pilot." These were, for the most part, pilots who had washed out of the Aviation Cadet Program; some were CPTP pilots and, later, also artillery officers who volunteered to fly. To the tune of the field artillery song, "The Caissons Go Rolling Along," this little ditty was sung over many a bottle of Lone Star beer:

> *Over clouds, under wires, to hell with landing gears and tires,*
> *We're the eyes of the Ar-til-lery,*
> *In and out through the trees, we're as hard to find as fleas,*
> *We're the eyes of the Ar-til-lery.*

> *CHORUS*
> *So it's fly, fly, and see for the Field Artillery;*
> *shout out your data loud and strong!*
> *We will give the Axis fits with our Maytag Messerschmitts,*
> *We're the Grasshopper Artillery.*

I can hear it now, "What's a caisson?" Only because my dad drove one in World War I can I give you an answer. A caisson was a wagon drawn by three teams of horses that carried the shells up to the big guns from the supply areas. For a kid from Brooklyn, my dad became a pretty good horse man.

WOOD DALE AIRPORT

O f the half dozen or so small airports that once surrounded the present O'Hare International Airport, Wood Dale Airport on Thorndale Road and Central Avenue probably was the most unique. Although all were special in their own ways, Wood Dale had the largest and most handsome-appearing hangar and administration buildings in the area, with the possible exception of Pal-Waukee Airport.

For the record, the other small airports that faded away as ORD blossomed were Ravenswood on Touhy Avenue east of York Road; Sky Haven near Grand Avenue and Wolf Road; Wilson Airport on Lawrence Avenue and River Road; American Airport at Devon and Higgins Road; and Park Ridge Airport at Touhy and River Roads.

Although the airport was thought to be opened sometime prior to World War II, the hangar and administration buildings were probably built when the U.S. Navy began operations there in 1942. When pilot training was expanded at Glenview Naval Air Station, fifteen satellite airfields were established around the northwest suburban area of Chicago. Of these fifteen, four became civilian airports after the war. They were Arlington Heights, Chicagoland at Half Day, Wood Dale and possibly Schaumburg (Roselle).

In 1946, the Moody Bible Institute began pilot and mechanic training for its missionaries at Elmhurst Airport in a Quonset hut on Lake Street near Route 83. Prior to this, the students had to be bussed to the field from the campus on Clark Street on Chicago's near North Side. When Commonwealth Edison decided it had to run a power line through the

Moody Bible Cub at Wood Dale Airport, 1950s. *Tribune.*

Park Ridge Airport at Touhy Avenue and River Road, 1941. *Finzer.*

middle of the airport, Elmhurst closed on New Year's Eve 1956. The school then moved to Wood Dale.

The small turf field at Wood Dale was ideal for the type of training needed for the missionaries. The runways were 1,800 and 2,700 feet long and rolling. The technical course covered four years. The principal studies the first two years were Bible and missionary subjects, an introduction to flying, radio and photography. The last two years were advanced flying through to

American Airport, also known as Heath Field, at Devon Avenue and Higgins Road, 1941. *Finzer.*

a commercial pilot's license. Seaplane ratings were earned at the Chicago Seaplane Base at the Navy Pier on the Chicago lakefront. The manager of the field was Paul Wertheimer, also a flight instructor and examiner who had been flying since 1929.

The program was started by former Baptist pastor and flight instructor Paul Robinson. Robinson learned to fly and had just soloed three days before the attack on Pearl Harbor. An early graduate of Moody, he had wanted to do missionary work in South America, but the war grounded most civilian flying. So he flew with the Civil Air Patrol until the war ended and gained a wealth of experience. Too old now for missionary work, he wanted to set up a school but lacked the backing. He was able to interest his former school, Moody, to finance the job.

An interesting concept was developed by one of the missionary "bush" pilots in South America and demonstrated on the Wood Dale field to the news media and military and civil aviation authorities. A canvas bag resembling a deep bucket was lowered at the end of 1,500 feet of heavy cord from a sixty-five-horsepower Piper Cub while it circled over a designated spot on the ground. As the Cub circled, the bucket became stationary, allowing equipment and or medical supplies to be delivered or picked up. Evidently, the pilot was flying perfect "on-pylon" turns over the spot, a standard commercial pilot maneuver.

The Moody school remained at Wood Dale until the growth of O'Hare International forced it to move to Elizabethton, Tennessee, in late 1967.

Wood Dale Airport, 1950s. *Tonkin.*

Apparently, Wood Dale was not exclusively used by the Moody school. In the late 1940s and early 1950s, the Chicago Glider Club conducted some soaring activities on the field. A couple slide photographs taken by Stan Tonkin, a resident of Wood Dale at the time, show at least two gliders and a fairly large group of people assembled on the west side of the field. In one photo, a red Waco biplane, likely a UPF-7, is either alighting or departing about fifty feet over the field. In the background of both photos is a farmhouse with a steep gabled roof with two dormers and a large barn. In the other photo, a green (blue?) and white Aeronca is seen aloft in the same area. A third photo depicts a white Luscombe Silvare, N71623, with red trim hitched to the back of a '49 Chevy two-door sedan. The wings of the Luscombe are on top of the car. There are remnants of snow on the ground, and the two-story hangar and *T* hangars are in the background. Perhaps the plane was being moved for major maintenance. Ken Flaglor and his brother were spark plugs of this glider club at the time. By the late 1950s, the club had split up, and Flaglor's group moved north to Chicagoland Airport while the other half moved to Ed Prosperi's Tinley Park Airfield, southwest of the city.

Ken Flaglor became a prominent member of the Experimental Aircraft Association (EAA), which was just being organized in the 1950s. He designed, built and flew several aircraft that would be considered ultra-lights or sport planes today. But probably his most ambitious project was a replica of one of the most exciting racing planes of the 1930s golden age of aviation, a Gee Bee (Granville Brothers) Model "Y" Senior Sportster. The original Sportster was flown in the 1933 National Air Races at the Curtiss Reynolds Airfield (later Glenview NAS) by one of the most remarkable but little-known female air racers, Florence Klingensmith. (Don't let the name fool you. She was a beautiful girl and one heck of a flyer!) Ken also built a smaller homebuilt racer, a Sonera designed by John Monett of Elgin, Illinois, in the 1970s. Ken was nice enough to take me for a ride in his Volkswagen engine–powered racer, which was a demonstration of his flying skill, as we were both far from being lightweights.

When the east–west runway was built at O'Hare, the Moody flight school was hemmed in by regulations. Its pilots had to stay one thousand feet above the nearby residents but below 1,500 feet to avoid O'Hare traffic. Soon after Moody moved to Tennessee, the property was sold to Sievert Klefstad, who developed Wood Dale's first industrial park there. So the residents of Wood Dale traded the noise of putt-putt airplanes for the roar of jet planes. That's progress.

Noise continues to be a problem to the residents around O'Hare, but at least they don't have to contend with an odor problem such as once plagued the Midway Airport neighborhood. An old-time Midway mechanic once told me that at one time all you had to do to determine the wind direction was to sniff the air. If the wind were from the northeast, the Chicago stockyards would let you know it; from the northwest, the Sanitary District made itself evident; and from the southwest, the corn products factory at Summit Argo was very distinctive. But the best was a southeast wind, which blew in over the Cracker Jack factory. He also told me that in the 1930s, when coal-burning furnaces were the norm, visibility was often as little as two miles on an otherwise clear day, and pilots in open-cockpit planes had to smell their way into Midway. That's progress, too!

INDEX

INDEX

INDEX

INDEX

ABOUT THE AUTHOR

Also the author of *Lost Airports of Chicago* with The History Press, Nick Selig has been a teenage Civil Air Patrol cadet; army aviation mechanic; civilian general aviation mechanic; Piper Cub flight instructor; instrument flight instructor and maintenance manager for a well-known nationwide flight school; charter, freight and corporate pilot; and an airline maintenance technician for twenty-one years. The best job he has ever held has been as the husband of a female pilot he met at Pal-Waukee Airport in the 1960s. As weekend flyers in their 1948 Stinson Flying Station Wagon, they came to realize that most of the small airports in the Chicago area had faded away without any fanfare but had played an important role in our nation's history. He decided to give them some recognition before they were completely forgotten. As you stroll your local shopping mall, housing development or industrial park, you might be walking on a former airfield. Heads up!